CENSORSHIP LITIGATION

and the Schools

Proceedings of a
Colloquium Held
January 1981

Office for Intellectual Freedom
American Library Association
Chicago 1983

Designed by Ellen Pettengell

Composed by Compositors in Melior
on an Autologic APS-5 Phototypesetting System

Printed on 50-pound Antique Glatfelter, a pH-neutral
stock, and bound in 10-point Carolina cover stock
by Cushing-Malloy, Inc.

Library of Congress Cataloging in Publication Data
Main entry under title:

Censorship litigation and the schools.

Proceedings of the Colloquium on School and
School Library Book Censorship Litigation,
held in Washington, D.C.
1. School libraries—United States—Censorship—
Congresses. 2. Libraries—Law and legislation—
United States—Congresses. 3. Text-books—United
States—Censorship—Congresses. I. Colloquium on
School and School Library Book Censorship
Litigation (1981 : Washington, D.C.)
Z675.S3C36 1982 025.2'1878'0973 82-24458
ISBN 0-8389-3279-7

CONTENTS

FOREWORD

It was early 1980 when consideration was first given to organizing a colloquium among attorneys and organizations active in opposing school-book censorship. At that time, the number and visibility of aggravated book censorship actions appeared to have markedly increased. In turn, the increased incidence of censorship led to more frequent litigation.

Too many of the cases opposing censorship had been "lost," while even the "successful" litigation failed to yield consistent or generally satisfactory legal precedent for application in future cases. No overall litigation strategy had been formulated. Indeed, the numerous anticensorship groups were often unaware of each other's activities, or they found themselves in disagreement over tactics or substantive approach.

In March 1980, as General Counsel to the Association of American Publishers, I wrote to the American Civil Liberties Union, by far the leading source of aid and counsel for anticensorship litigants, proposing the organization of a "high-level strategy session" on schoolbook censorship litigation. Copies of that proposal were sent to the American Library Association, the Association of American Publishers, and the Freedom to Read Foundation, all leading amicus curiae groups dedicated to advancing freedom of expression and First Amendment principles in America's schools and libraries. Positive discussions commenced, but the effort was put on hold to await further developments in three very important cases—Zykan[1] in the Seventh Circuit and Pico[2] and Bicknell[3] in the Second—then still pending on appeal.

In August 1980 Zykan was decided, with a divided Seventh Circuit panel dismissing the plaintiffs' complaint (albeit subject to repleading) and defining what appeared to be quite restrictive standards for federal judicial intervention to prevent schoolbook censorship. Then, in early October, the Pico and Bicknell cases were decided, with a sharply divided Second Circuit panel setting somewhat more liberal standards but nonetheless dismissing Bicknell's claims by a two to one margin while remanding the Pico case for trial.

The time was now right. Within days ACLU, AAP, ALA, and FtRF approved a proposal to mount a colloquium in late January 1981, and the Playboy Foundation pledged $5,000 as seed money. Three months of intensive preparations followed. Happily, despite the relatively short lead time, all aspects of the colloquium came together smoothly. Generous additional funding, sufficient to defray colloquium expenses, pay honoraria, and provide modest financial support for needy attendees, was secured from the Gannett Newspaper Foundation, Doubleday and Company, Random House, the Freedom to Read Foundation, Macmillan, and Harper and Row, Publishers. Three eminent scholars and attorneys were commissioned to produce formal papers, and these were distributed before the colloquium. Numerous other interested organizations agreed to prepare briefer status reports for distribution at the colloquium. An impressive roster of guest panelists was developed, and more than fifty other participants, representing most of the litigants and leading interest groups in the field, agreed to attend.

The colloquium was a success, but the sparkling level of discussion by no means resolved the many complex and ambiguous legal, political, and constitutional issues presented. All seemed to agree that schoolbook censorship cases will be extremely difficult to win and that no ready or easy theoretical solution is likely to be found. All also agreed that coordination, cooperation, and sustained effort among pro-First Amendment attorneys and organizations is absolutely essential.

The fast pace of developments since late January 1981 simply reaffirms the lessons of the colloquium. In March 1981 an evenly divided Second Circuit Court refused (by a five to five vote) to grant the school board's petition for rehearing in banc in the Pico case. Then in May the Island Trees school board petitioned the Supreme Court for certiorari. In early October 1981 the Supreme Court granted the petition and in June 1982, in a five to four decision, found against the school board, remanding the case to a lower court. The majority of the court expressed diverse reasons for their finding, but the plurality opinion was widely regarded as a victory for proponents of intellectual freedom.

These developments were paralleled by massive media coverage of the stepped-up activities of the Moral Majority and other right-wing groups around the nation. A creationist group's challenge to the California Board of Education policy on evolution in biology textbooks was tried to an inconclusive result before national network news coverage. In March the General Assembly of Arkansas enacted, and the state's governor signed, a creationism act designed to impose "equal time" for creationism in classrooms and in textbooks whenever evolution is taught in the public schools. As many as eighteen other states enacted or were considering similar legislation. Thereafter, in late May 1981 the American Civil Liberties Union brought an action challenging the constitutionality of the Arkansas act. The ACLU case was tried in December 1981, again to intensive attention in the national media.

Henry R. Kaufman

PUBLISHER'S NOTE

The transcript of proceedings which follows is an abridged version of what was said by participants at the Colloquium on School and School Library Book Censorship Litigation. The text was edited by Naomi Donson. Notes and citations have been added.

LIST OF PARTICIPANTS

Floyd Abrams, partner, Cahill, Gordon & Reindel, New York City.

Alex P. Allain, special counsel, Freedom to Read Foundation.

Stephen Arons, director, Legal Studies, University of Massachusetts.

Frank Askin, associated with the Rutgers Constitutional Litigation Clinic; general counsel, American Civil Liberties Union; professor, Rutgers School of Law.

Michael A. Bamberger, general counsel, Media Coalition; partner, Finley, Kumble, Wagner, Heine & Underberg, New York City.

Howard R. Besser, Ohio Civil Liberties Union, counsel in *Minarcini v. Strongsville City School District.*

Vincent Blasi, professor, University of Michigan Law School.

Stephen E. Borofsky, counsel in *Salvail v. Nashua Board of Education.*

Ann Brick, Howard, Prim, Rice, Nemerouski, Canady & Pollack, San Francisco, counsel in *Wexner v. Anderson Union High School.*

Daniel W. Casey, member, Board of Trustees of the Freedom to Read Foundation; public library trustee, Syracuse, New York.

Jerry Simon Chasen, Greenbaum, Wolff & Ernst, New York City; counsel, P.E.N. American Center.

Joan Collett, treasurer, Freedom to Read Foundation; director, St. Louis Public Library.

John C. Culver, former U.S. Senator from Iowa.

Norman Dorsen, professor, New York University School of Law; president, American Civil Liberties Union.

Robert P. Doyle, assistant to the director, Office for Intellectual Freedom, American Library Association.

Rob Eggert, Student Press Law Center, Washington, D.C.

Victoria B. Eiger, staff attorney, American Jewish Congress.

Arthur Eisenberg, staff attorney, New York Civil Liberties Union.

Bruce J. Ennis, national legal director, American Civil Liberties Union.

Ira Glasser, executive director, American Civil Liberties Union.

Jeremiah Gutman, president, New York Civil Liberties Union.

Charles Halpern, director, Institute for Public Representation; associate professor, Georgetown University Legal Center.

Mary Hutchings Reed, Sidley & Austin, Chicago; counsel, American Library Association.

Burton Joseph, chair, Playboy Foundation; member, Board of Trustees, Freedom to Read Foundation.

Michelle Marder Kamhi, research consultant, American Library Association and the Association of American Publishers.

Leanne Katz, coordinator, National Coalition Against Censorship.

Henry R. Kaufman, former general counsel, Association of American Publishers; attorney now in private practice, New York City.

Richard P. Kleeman, senior vice-president, Association of American Publishers; staff director, AAP Freedom to Read Committee; member, Board of Trustees, Freedom to Read Foundation.

Joel Klein, partner, Rogovin, Stern & Huge, Washington, D.C.

James Klenk, Reuben and Proctor, Chicago; counsel, Freedom to Read Foundation.

Judith F. Krug, executive director, Freedom to Read Foundation; director, Office for Intellectual Freedom, American Library Association.

Frederick S. Le Clerq, professor, University of Tennessee; counsel to the National Association of Biology Teachers in *Daniel* v. *Waters* and *Steele* v. *Waters*.

Alan Levine, former staff lawyer, New York Civil Liberties Union; partner, Clark, Wolf, Levine & Paratis, New York City; counsel in *Presidents Council District 25* v. *Community School Board No. 25* and *Board of Education, Island Trees Union Free School District* v. *Pico*.

Dorothy Massie, staff member, Teacher Rights Division, National Educational Association.

Kenneth D. McCormick, Doubleday & Co.; former chair, Association of American Publishers' Freedom to Read Committee.

Florence McMullin, president, Freedom to Read Foundation; anticensorship lobbyist in Washington state.

Edward A. Miller, vice-president and general counsel, Harper & Row; chairman, Lawyers' Committee, Association of American Publishers.

Wayne A. Moyer, executive director, National Association of Biology Teachers.

Kenneth P. Norwick, partner, Norwick, Raggio, Jaffe & Kayser, New York City; active with the New York Civil Liberties Union and in the publishing field.

Robert M. O'Neil, law professor and president, University of Wisconsin.

Susanne Oychez, former research assistant for Professor Robert M. O'Neil.

Frank R. Parker, Lawyers' Committee for Civil Rights Under the Law, Jackson, Miss.; counsel in *Loewen* v. *Turnipseed*.

Stephen L. Pevar, staff attorney, American Civil Liberties Union; counsel in *Fogarty* v. *Atchley*.

Barbara Phillips, Lawyers' Committee for Civil Rights Under the Law, Jackson, Miss.

Robert Posch, counsel, Doubleday & Co.

David Rabban, counsel, American Association of University Professors.

Henry Reichman, assistant director, Office for Intellectual Freedom, American Library Association; deputy executive director, Freedom to Read Foundation.

R. Bruce Rich, Weil, Gotshal & Manges, New York City; counsel, Association of American Publishers' Freedom to Read Committee.

Anthony M. Schulte, executive vice-president, Random House; chair, Association of American Publishers' Freedom to Read Committee.

Jonathan Shapiro, Stern and Shapiro, Newton, Mass.; counsel, *Right to Read Committee* v. *School Committee of the City of Chelsea.*

Diane Shugert, chair, Committee Against Censorship, National Council of Teachers of English.

Charles Sims, national staff counsel, American Civil Liberties Union.

James R. Squire, senior vice-president, Ginn & Co.; member, Association of American Publishers' Freedom to Read Committee.

Elizabeth Stone, vice-president, American Library Association; trustee, Freedom to Read Foundation.

William Van Alstyne, professor of constitutional law, Duke University.

Mark G. Yudof, professor specializing in education matters, University of Texas Law School.

FIRST GENERAL SESSION

After some welcoming remarks, Anthony M. Schulte, Chair of the Association of American Publishers' Freedom to Read Committee, launched the proceedings.

Anthony Schulte:

We are here to talk about restraints in circulation or dissemination of books and curricular materials in schools and libraries. This issue has become more and more important from the First Amendment point of view to book publishers.

This growing concern over schoolbook censorship reflects the interests of schoolbook publishers as well as publishers overall, since our association covers the full range of publishing from textbook to general trade book publishing. We have been involved with the gathering of information through a national survey of administrators, principals, and district and local librarians in public schools throughout the country. We believe that this survey is the broadest ever done to determine just how much interference there actually is with school and library book selection and circulation and its impact on the educational apparatus. The preliminary findings are extremely interesting. Since they are based on information gathered during May of 1980, I think we can all assume that the situation has not eased up, given the recent political turn of events.

Norman Dorsen:

In thinking about the colloquium, I could not help but reflect on where these school censorship issues stand in the overall context of the ACLU's work and the civil liberties problems confronting the country. Everyone knows that today we are faced with intense problems of sex discrimination, race discrimination, reproductive freedom, and a wide range of First

1

Amendment issues. We are entering a particularly difficult period with issues such as school prayer, that we thought had been dealt with almost two decades ago, again coming to the fore.

So the question is, How important is this? Ultimately it is an analogue to the biology truism that you are what you eat. If that is true, it is also true in the intellectual sense, and even morally, that you are what you read. And what you read as a child is largely what people present to you and permit you to read. For that reason, the issues here have particular importance from the special perspective of the ACLU.

Brandeis once said that he held the highest office in the land, and he said that before he became a Justice of the Supreme Court of the United States. He meant that he was a citizen. From the ACLU's perspective, each citizen is sovereign and each citizen's well-being and personal integrity are what we are in business to protect. Our job is to make sure each citizen, each sovereign, each child, is given the opportunity to read and to learn in a way that does not impair his or her natural growth and is permitted to develop his or her potential. Beyond that, this issue concerns the tone and nature of society as a whole. If each person is sovereign, it is also true that what happens in the school and how each person develops suffuses the society and develops it in new directions.

The issues are important, but it is also relevant to know that they are very difficult. And it is very easy, especially in a group of this kind, to be glib, to be flag waving in the sense that we're for the First Amendment, we're for freedom of speech, we're the advocates of whatever is going to be most open in society. But there are, as usual, countervailing factors. Obviously the first problem is that the issues have to be resolved in the context of a functioning, workable educational system. The papers prepared for the colloquium by Bob O'Neil and Mark Yudof identify some of the problems of those systems and the problem of reconciling our concerns with the operation of the school system. This leads to the second difficulty, and that is establishing to our own satisfaction—and that means ultimately to the court's satisfaction—a coherent intellectual theory, one that can be defended to people who do not share all our premises. It is very easy to convince those who do. But to appear before judges who start from premises indifferent to, or even antithetical to, our premises and to persuade them requires coherence, subtlety, and sophistication.

Burton Joseph:

When we decided to convene this colloquium, we specifically decided to have a small group in which everyone could make a unique contribution. Each participant has a special interest and a unique experience to contribute. We can learn from each other.

Current Social and Political Trends and Their Implications for Future Litigation

Robert M. O'Neil

It is easy to forget how recent is the development of law dealing with textbook and curricular censorship. The Queens school district ban on circulation of Piri Thomas' *Down These Mean Streets*, which brought the issue into court for the first time, took place barely ten years ago.[1] There had been a few legal skirmishes before the 1970s—an abortive challenge in the 1940s by several Jewish parents concerned about ethnic stereotypes in *Oliver Twist* and *The Merchant of Venice*,[2] and a Baltimore teacher's vain plea for reinstatement following his dismissal for assigning *Brave New World*.[3] But none of the earlier cases remotely addressed the central issues with which we are now concerned—the issues which Justices Douglas and Stewart, dissenting from the denial of *certiorari* in the *Down These Mean Streets* case,[4] believed the Supreme Court must eventually face.

While the Supreme Court has not yet accepted that challenge, the lower courts have developed a substantial body of pertinent law. The cases follow three phases or cycles. First, there was only the *Down These Mean Streets* case, with its callous refusal to recognize even the possibility of a First Amendment interest in library collections. The law remained in that sorry state for four years, until the Sixth Circuit Federal Court of Appeals (in the Strongsville, Ohio, case) took a boldly different view of the constitutional claims.[5] That decision was soon reinforced by two similar judgments against school boards in Nashua, New Hampshire,[6] and Chelsea, Massachusetts.[7]

The third and latest phase of censorship litigation has been more like the first. The decisions in cases from Warsaw, Indiana;[8] Island Trees, New York;[9] and Vergennes, Vermont,[10] have brought a mixture of confusion and dismay to those who believed the law had found its proper course after Strongsville. Such dissonance among federal appeals courts often invites Supreme Court review, and quite possibly a grant of *certiorari* in one of the current cases would provide useful clarification. But time would now be better spent on anticipating the cases of the next decade rather than on conjecturing how the Supreme Court might resolve issues it has managed for the past decade to avoid. In fact, by the time the Supreme

Court does get around to reviewing the censorship issue, the locus of litigation in the lower courts may well have shifted dramatically so that a Supreme Court decision in one of the more familiar cases may have limited value.

In order to speculate about the future course of litigation in this area, four model situations might be posited: First, we might look at the "noncirculation" case—the decision not to circulate material already in a collection, but for reasons not readily amenable to the legal challenges developed in the earlier cases. Second, we might pose the "nonacquisition" case—the more difficult situation involving an initial judgment not to acquire controversial material. Third, moving from the library to the classroom, we might examine the "questionable adoption" situation—the decision to adopt, approve, or assign controversial material. Fourth, and finally, we might consider the "curricular modification" situation—the deletion or major modification of a course for reasons that may invite legal challenge. Although the first two situations chiefly involve the library and the other two the classroom, there will be some unavoidable crossover of principles among the four situations, with possibly resulting confusion. Decisions made by school officials often affect both library and classroom; not only are the resulting legal claims of teachers and librarians somewhat parallel, but the effects upon students of library and classroom censorship are even more clearly concurrent. Thus the necessarily artificial separation among the four prototype situations imperfectly reflects many realities of the educational world.[11]

THE NONCIRCULATION SITUATION

Most of the cases to date have involved noncirculation decisions based upon politically conservative objections to content. Parent groups typically bring pressure upon school boards or administrators, who in turn tell librarians not to circulate, or teachers not to assign, a challenged work. The courts are then asked to find the removal violative of First Amendment rights of students and/or teachers (and occasionally of a librarian) and to restore the work to the shelves. Problems of proving motive or rationale may be substantial in such cases, and the courts have shown variant willingness to presume a constitutionally improper reason for the removal of controversial material. But the basic issue in this classic removal case is clear enough.

There is, however, a growing concern in the noncirculation area about pressures from a quite different quarter—from what have often been termed "the would-be censors of the Left." Several recent incidents invite at least apprehension, if not alarm. The Council on Interracial Books for Children and its rating instrument have aroused much anxiety in library circles.[12] The decision several years ago of the New Trier,

Illinois, school board to remove *Huckleberry Finn* from the required reading lists because some black parents objected to the character of "Nigger Jim";[13] or the black community pressure in Oakland, California, which caused the school board to remove *Daddy Was a Numbers Runner* from the junior high school libraries;[14] or the action of the Montgomery County, Maryland, public library in withdrawing from the shelves a book labeled "sexist" by the National Organization of Women;[15] and the narrowly averted removal of several allegedly racist and sexist materials from the Cedar Rapids, Iowa, libraries a couple of years ago—these and other recent incidents suggest that the concern over "censorship from the Left" deserves attention. The time will surely come when groups committed to protection of intellectual freedom must decide whether these pressures should be resisted in court, even at the risk of misunderstanding by many who share views on affirmative action and equal opportunity. The basic issue—one which has been with us before in uncomfortable contexts like Skokie and *Birth of a Nation*—is whether the First Amendment views acts of censorship less critically when their basis is the protection of women and minorities.

The answer must, of course, come at two levels. In terms of pure constitutional law, there can be no difference between the school board that removes *Huckleberry Finn* or *Daddy Was a Numbers Runner* and the board that bans *One Flew over the Cuckoo's Nest* or *Cat's Cradle*. Content-based censorship of legally protected works is intolerable regardless of the underlying motive or purpose. Yet not all acts of censorship need be challenged with equal vigor. While the removal of allegedly racist and sexist materials must be resisted (as did the Iowa Civil Liberties Union in the Cedar Rapids case), the impetus to litigate the issue might be tempered by circumstances. Moreover, the incidence of "censorship from the Left" is likely to be relatively limited and confined largely to communities like Montgomery County and New Trier. Perhaps groups committed both to freedom of expression and to equality of opportunity can perform a valuable mediating role in such cases by keeping them out of court, if possible. In principle, however, there is no doubt that such groups should be as willing to seek protection for *Huckleberry Finn* as for *Catch-22*.

To this point we have treated noncirculation decisions entirely as administrative edicts. But suppose the book is withheld not by the decree of a censorious board but by the librarian's own hand. Such a case has not yet reached the courts, but surely it cannot be too far away. Indeed it is reported that such a case almost developed in Little Rock, Arkansas, a couple of years ago. A librarian apparently decided that a recently acquired work would be a bit too spicy for a group of teenage patrons, and thus denied them access to it. The students approached the Civil Liberties Union, which considered but eventually declined to pursue the matter.

This kind of noncirculation case is of course quite different in several ways from the classic case with which we began. To the patron, the result is identical, but that is where the similarity ends. The operative judgment in this case reflects the professional expertise of a person trained in the field. Indeed, a noncirculation decision by a professional librarian may well involve the exercise of First Amendment rights as significant as the patron's own claim of access. Thus, to assimilate the crude school board ban and the librarian's considered restraint and call them both "censorship," as the Little Rock students may have done, largely misses the point.

There is no law that really resolves this perplexing kind of case. There is, however, one unreported federal district court decision in 1972 that offers a starting point. A schoolteacher in a Columbus, Ohio, suburb ordered for her class copies of Edgar Lee Masters' *Spoon River Anthology*, but before giving them to the students she removed four short poems. The excised verses, she believed, were too mature for her class; at least as far as the facts of the case show, no pressure was brought upon her by the principal or even the department chairman (both of whom had earlier approved assignment of the unexpurgated anthology).

The district court recognized the novelty of the case, but resolved the issue against the students on essentially jurisdictional grounds.[16] Since students were not ultimately denied access to the censored pages, the court found no First Amendment violation; the opinion contains just the barest hint that a finding in the students' favor might actually infringe First Amendment rights of the *teacher*.

The *Spoon River* case, despite its failure to resolve the constitutional issue, at least refines the dilemma of the "noncirculation" hypothetical. Courts should be very slow to intervene in such a situation—at least if the professional judgment of the librarian is truly unfettered and is not simply capitulation to adminstrative or board pressure. In such a case a broad range of professional discretion should be recognized within which librarians may decide whether or not to circulate material, even at the risk of denying some patrons access to legally protected works. The risks of judicial intervention in a case of truly untrammeled professional judgment far outweigh the possible benefits, even where the librarian's action is unmistakably "censorship."

THE NONACQUISITION SITUATION

Much of the analysis in this field of law has been distorted by the practical difference between the decision not to circulate a work already on the shelf and the decision not to acquire that same work. Several courts have suggested that recognition of a remedy in the former situation would open the floodgates to claims of the latter type, and for that reason have been inhospitable to both. Indeed, even among those responsible for the direction of anticensorship litigation, concern about the nonacquisition case has confounded planning and strategy.

Legally, the differences may be less important than they appear. Recall, for example, the Strongsville, Ohio, case, in which the court of appeals found unconstitutional not only the school board's *removal* of certain existing works but its ban on the *purchase* of others. While that court may well have carried the argument too far in other respects, its willingness to treat certain noncirculation and nonacquisition decisions essentially alike seems quite logical. Of course, the assimilation of the two claims was made much easier by the linking in time of two such actions, reflecting the same constitutionally impermissible motive. Much more difficult are cases in which the two acts occur separately, or in which the motive or purpose for a negative decision is less clear.

As a practical matter, most nonacquisition decisions are those of the individual librarian or professional staff. Rarely will a school or library board order that certain works not be acquired, unless of course a legally vulnerable objection to content or to the politics of the author underlies such action. Typically, where the board orders the library staff to reduce acquisitions by twenty percent to meet a budget crisis, no constitutional claim arises. Even where a board sets policy with greater specificity than simply the limits of the budget—for example, emphasizing some areas of content and deemphasizing others—no constitutional infringement would seem to exist. Only where the board policy is highly selective—down to the individual author or work as in the Strongsville or Nashua cases, for example—could a constitutional claim be mounted. Thus, as a practical matter the only nonacquisition decisions that are likely to be subjects for legal challenge are those made by individual librarians or library staffs.

There may by many grounds for a negative acquisition decision, some of which surely create no constitutional problem. Such criteria as cost, potential student and teacher interest, available space, duplication of existing collections, probable longevity, and the like are well within the scope of a librarian's discretion. Not only is consideration of such factors legally permissible; it is in fact a major basis of the claim for First Amendment protection for professional librarianship. Some discretion must be exercised, and the relevant criteria are those in which librarians are most expert.

Slightly more difficult is the case in which a librarian declines to acquire a book on essentially legal grounds. If, for example, the content could be thought obscene, or might incite readers to violence, the librarian would presumably be allowed to apply such content standards even in the absence of a binding court decision. Surely, given the risks of making an erroneous judgment, the librarian should be allowed to err on the side of caution. (There are risks in carrying this theory too far; the line between the librarian's judgment and that of the principal or school board may not always be clear. Where in fact the librarian is doing the administrator's bidding with regard to a possibly obscene book, the claim of professional responsibility and judgment of course becomes attenuated.)

As a variant, consider the librarian who seeks to avoid a controversy of a different sort—declining, for instance, to buy for the library a creationist biology textbook after the courts have held its classroom use to violate the establishment clause. One may argue that such books belong in the library, even though their use in the classroom is forbidden— indeed, that the school may best respond to the wishes of deeply religious parents by making sure such works are accessible to the library despite their unavailability as instructional materials. Yet the librarian might well err on the side of caution in feeling that the buying of creationist materials would violate the spirit, if not the letter, of the establishment clause.

To summarize with regard to the nonacquisition situation: Highly selective board policies reflecting impermissible content (or author) judgments are without doubt legally vulnerable, and as the Strongsville case indicates, judicial relief in such uncommon cases should not open the floodgates to frivolous nonacquisition claims. Apart from the negative board policy that reflects a constitutionally impermissible rationale, the only other nonacquisition decisions that should be litigated are those that reveal outrageous bias on the part of a librarian or professional staff. Obviously cases of this sort will be extremely rare, and the prospect of judicial intervention therefore remains quite remote. Indeed, the very improbability and infrequency of such cases is what makes appropriate the recognition of nonacquisition as a possible forum for judicial review.

THE "QUESTIONABLE ADOPTION" SITUATION

Let us assume at the outset that *positive* acquisition decisions may never be challenged—that is, it would be unthinkable to enjoin on constitutional grounds the decision of board or library to buy a particular book. Even the most blatantly pornographic work, with the least redeeming value, should be immune until and unless it is circulated—and even then, in many states, exceptions to the obscenity laws would protect a librarian from legal liability. Thus as a practical matter, legal challenge to a single acquisition decision need not be considered.

The case is much less clear, however, with regard to curricular materials. Several kinds of challenges can be envisioned, and at least three such have made their way through the courts. We might initially put aside the interesting suits in West Virginia[17] and Texas[18] disputing the adoption of teaching materials allegedly violative of the First Amendment's establishment clause because they favored "secular humanism." Much more could be said on this intriguing topic, but not here.

Mention of religion does, however, bring to the fore another case which came at the issue from the other side. The West Clark, Indiana, school board had adopted from the state-approved list a text called *Biology: A Search for Order*. A group of parents brought suit and successfully argued that the adoption of an avowedly creationist textbook was an impermissible "establishment" of religion.[19] The case was not without its difficulties, however. When the Indiana Civil Liberties Union sought permission from the national organization to bring suit on behalf of the anti-creationist parents, there was much concern about the precedent of asking a court to ban a book, however objectionable its content. The internal dilemma was eventually resolved in favor of religious freedom, but with lingering concern about the implications for liberty of expression. The prospect of judicial censorship, to put the suit in its worst light, is an awesome one for persons committed to intellectual freedom. Yet the alternative, perhaps even less palatable, would be to have schoolchildren learn only the Genesis theory of the origins of human life. If the local board or the state legislature had banned outright the teaching of Darwinism, or even punished a teacher for presenting both sides of the issue, judicial intervention would of course have been appropriate and the outcome clear since the Supreme Court's 1968 decision striking down state antievolution laws. In effect, the West Clark case was really no different; the complication stemmed from the form of judicial relief sought to enjoin a clear violation of the establishment clause.

The other case deals with race rather than religion. Although state law permitted as many as five options, the Mississippi State Textbook Commission had for years approved only a single history text. That book presented a quite traditional, some might say archaic, view of the role of blacks in the state's history. The commission had rejected alternative works which gave fuller and fairer treatments of the racial question. The authors of one of the competing texts and other educators and students brought suit in the federal court to enjoin the single adoption on grounds both of racial equality and intellectual freedom. They also sought judicial *imprimatur* for the competing work. The court went part way with the plaintiffs, holding that the current procedure violated First Amendment freedoms and that the adoption of the archaic text evidenced a racially discriminatory purpose.[20] But the court declined to intervene in the textbook selection process any further than necessary to decide the claim at hand. In framing its limited relief, the court recognized the hazards of broader intervention in the complex process of textbook selection and review.

These cases do not exhaust the full range of possible controversy. For example, there have been suggestions of growing urgency that certain teaching materials are impermissibly sexist and should be barred or removed, even though the constitutional basis for such a claim remains uncertain.[21] Here, too, many civil libertarians are uncomfortable simply about asking a judge to ban a book. The precedent thus created may later return to haunt those who have created it. Yet the costs of being unwilling to litigate such issues are also substantial, and in the long run probably more so—white children as well as black denied an unbiased view of racial tensions in Mississippi history, and Indiana pupils given only the Genesis view of life's origins. Resort to the courts should be made sparingly in such cases, and (as both judges recognized in framing their decrees) the scope of relief should be limited to enjoining the particular unconstitutional adoption.

Other situations will be less clear. There will undoubtedly be growing pressure for "equal time" on the origins of life issue, and texts presenting both the creationist and evolutionary theories may be increasingly popular in conservative areas. Such materials may not fully reflect current scientific learning, but are not for that reason constitutionally defective. The judge in the West Clark case enjoined the use of *Biology: A Search for Order* only because it gave a quite biased, one-sided view of the origins of life. Had the Mississippi history text been better balanced, even though less than fully appreciative of the contribution of blacks to the state's development, the court would probably have declined to act. It is only the extreme cases that warrant such intervention.

THE CURRICULAR MODIFICATION SITUATION

Perhaps the most difficult situation of all involves a school board decision not to remove a book from the library or even to adopt one for the classroom, but to revise the curriculum. Two recent cases involve variations of that theme. The Warsaw, Indiana, case presents the question squarely, for among the challenged school board actions was the cancellation of courses in Black Literature, Gothic Literature, Folklore and Legend, and Science Fiction. The Adams-Arapahoe (Colorado) case may also pose the curricular modification issue, though less clearly; the board's decision to approve nearly 1300 teacher-recommended titles while refusing approval of ten specific books reflected as much a judgment about curriculum as about the books themselves.[22]

We might begin our analysis with the easiest case, the one least appropriate for judicial relief: the teacher-created curricular modification. Whether or not secondary teachers enjoy academic freedom comparable to that of college professors (of which more a bit later), there is little doubt that teachers, like librarians, should be left largely free by the courts to exercise professional judgment and discretion. Thus if a teacher selects one course approach rather than another, courts should intervene only in situations of clear constitutional violation of the West Clark type.

The harder questions concern board or administrative curricular modification, often contrary to teacher recommendations. The Supreme Court has spoken repeatedly of the need for judicial deference to local school authorities, and has warned lower courts they must not become "super school boards."[23] In striking down the West Virginia flag salute law many years ago, the court in a footnote seemed to sanction inculcation of patriotic values through the curriculum. Only last year, in holding that New York could require public school teachers to be United States citizens, the Supreme Court added, "A state properly may regard all teachers as having an obligation to promote civic virtues and understanding in their classes, regardless of the subjects taught."[24] Thus it is difficult to envision a broad constitutional challenge to the authority of local school boards over the curriculum, even where its exercise may be value biased.

Another line of Supreme Court thinking further complicates the issue. In striking down the Arkansas antievolution law, Justice Black added his concurring view that "it would be difficult to make a First Amendment case out of a state law eliminating the subject of higher mathematics, or astronomy, or biology from its curriculum."[25] Justice Stewart, in another separate concurrence, elaborated a bit: "A state is entirely free, for example, to decide that the only foreign language to be taught in its public schools shall be Spanish."[26] For him the Constitution would be violated only if state law forbade a teacher to tell his or her students that other languages existed—and that, in Justice Stewart's view, was precisely what Arkansas had done with respect to evolution.

Against this background, it is not easy to find a justiciable claim in the modification of the Warsaw elective curriculum, whatever the board's motives. Let us assume that the school board eliminated Gothic Literature because it did not like the kinds of books that had been assigned and believed that Warsaw children should be sheltered from such suggestive or salacious materials. If that goal could not be accomplished directly—by banning legally protected works on avowedly content grounds—may it nonetheless be accomplished indirectly? That is the intriguing issue on which the Warsaw and Colorado cases touch, but do not fully develop. It is an issue with which we will very likely be increasingly faced, if reports of "back to basics" movements in many conservative communities accurately reflect the course of curricular change.

Apart from the legal difficulties of mounting such a challenge, there are also practical barriers: Who, for example, is sufficiently aggrieved (in a legal sense) by the elimination of one course and the addition of another? To what extent would a court second-guess the board's judgment that budget, or student interest, or community needs, better justified one course than another? And, if a court were to require the continuation of a deleted course, what should be the extent and duration of relief? Until adequate answers to these and other tactical questions are clear, litigation over curricular modification seems a rather unfruitful pursuit. Thus in this context as in others, the exercise of the greater power (eliminating the course) may well subsume a lesser act (removing a book) that could not be achieved directly.

One consistent principle of accommodation is implied by the juxtaposition of the Colorado and Warsaw cases. The district judge in the Colorado case suggested that while the school board could have eliminated the senior Comparative Literature course entirely, it could not tamper on content grounds with the reading list so long as the course remained in the curriculum.[27] An elected school board does enjoy substantial latitude in setting the curriculum and in changing it. If a district chooses to offer only basic subjects, teachers in that district will enjoy quite limited freedom of expression. If, on the other hand, the school board decides to enrich the curriculum by offering advanced courses in drama, literature, government, and other complex and possibly controversial subjects, it must bear the consequences. Instructors hired to teach such courses properly enjoy a measure of intellectual freedom not available to their colleagues in manual training, home economics, and typing. Thus the school board can to a substantial degree adjust the scope of academic freedom available within the system—not by silencing a particular teacher because it dislikes what he says in class or the books he assigns, but rather by eliminating the course that is the catalyst for controversy. If it so acts, the school board too must accept the consequences—for example, complaints from parents who believe their children will do less well on college admissions tests if they can no longer take Comparative Literature or Problems of Democracy. Redress against curricular modification, in other words, should be political rather than judicial; if the school board can delete controversial courses and still be reelected, then that is what the community wants and the courts should not gainsay that judgment.

CONCLUSION: SOME UNFINISHED BUSINESS

The review of the four model situations, and their variants, leaves several loose threads. For one, the need remains to establish through litigation some protection for the librarian's First Amendment claims. Although librarians have several times been among the plaintiffs, none of the courts has seen any need to give constitutional protection to the exercise of the librarian's professional judgment. (In fact, only in the Vergennes, Vermont, case was the librarian's claim even separately considered, and there it was disposed of quite mechanically and summarily.)[28] Much has been said elsewhere about the two possible bases of the librarian's claim—the derivative interest in facilitating the patron's right of access to protected material, and the direct performance of activities which themselves may claim First Amendment protection.[29] These arguments have not been well developed in the cases, and therefore have not really been rejected by the courts. The need to advance and establish them should intensify during the next decade.

Second among the unfinished business is the "floodgate" issue on which we touched earlier. Some courts are understandably fearful that they may be inundated with lawsuits if they are the least bit receptive to book removal claims. That concern stems in part from some rather unguarded language in the Strongsville case—suggesting that unlawful censorship will be presumed in the absence of a content-neutral reason for removing a book. Taken literally, that formula would forbid a librarian from making room on finite shelves for more current or popular works by selling obsolete materials, for surely judgments about currency and popularity are not entirely content neutral. But the court could not have meant thus to hobble the exercise of the very judgment which its holding vindicated. Some clarification is urgent, but the Island Trees and Warsaw decisions surely do not provide it. In future litigation, what is needed is a new and more balanced approach to the floodgate issue—one which minimizes the prospect rather than avoiding it.

Third, there needs to be developed better criteria for challenging actions like the adoption of the Indiana biology text and the Mississippi history book. These two cases seem in retrospect relatively easy, and the results compatible with First Amendment principles. But the next cases—challenges, for example, to allegedly "sexist" classroom materials—may be less clear and the hazards of judicial intervention more serious.

Finally, among the "loose ends" to which further attention might be given, the basic nature of the teacher's constitutional claim needs to be better formulated. Even the most ardent teacher-rights proponent would probably agree that elementary and secondary school instructors are not exactly like university professors, and that some dimensions of academic freedom diminish as one moves from graduate school to the younger grades. Yet the challenge posed some five years ago by Professor Stephen Goldstein has never been answered; for him, academic freedom existed for a junior college business education instructor but not for the teacher of a twelfth-grade elective course in Comparative Literature.[30] There are differences, and not all the liberties enjoyed by university professors are appropriate even for high school teachers. The district judge in the Colorado case came closer than any other court by recognizing that the choosing of books for a twelfth-grade literature course should be part of a teacher's academic freedom, even if that freedom was neither complete nor coextensive with that of the university professor.[31] But the district judge stopped there, without drawing the boundaries—and then the appellate court came along with a wholly different view of secondary school governance. So the issue remains quite open. In fact, few aspects of censorship litigation are more central than the recognition of a teacher's constitutional right to teach and a librarian's constitutional right to acquire and circulate controversial materials.

The purpose of this paper has been much more to raise questions than to provide answers. A few responses have been suggested—at least in terms of general directions in which future litigation should or should not develop. The hope is that the description and the brief analysis of the four model situations, going largely beyond the issues that have already been resolved, will suggest future litigation strategies. If we are prepared at this volatile period in the evolution of the law of intellectual freedom to make some preliminary choices, we will then be better equipped to handle the real cases that will undoubtedly bring these now hypothetical questions to us.

General Directions of Future Litigation, a Panel Discussion

Panelists: Robert M. O'Neil, Ira Glasser, Judith F. Krug, J. Charles Park, and John Culver

THE POLITICAL CONTEXT

Henry Kaufman:

Bob O'Neil has given us a framework, within which we can think about all of these problems. What the panel will give us, I believe, is some sense of the political milieu in which we are working, of what is actually happening, and what may be likely to happen, in light of the current climate.

Mr. Culver:

I believe that Bob has done an excellent job describing the various conflicts that have emerged in the last ten years in this area. And I certainly want to commend him for demonstrating the complexity of the situation as well as the competing claims and values that are confronted in this context. Now I would like to offer some brief observations about the political trends which are likely to shape the nature, the climate, and the environment of future litigation. I believe Bob is correct in noting that the pressures of censorship arise on both the right as well as the left of the political spectrum. But as a practical matter, I believe the 1980s will see the strongest and most real impetus come from the Right. And this, I would submit, is the case for at least three reasons.

First, there is generally a degree of ambivalence, at least, to censorship moves from the Left, politically speaking. Most liberals, according to the commonly accepted meaning, oppose racism and sexism. But they also generally subscribe to a broad commitment and definition of free speech. There is an inherent tension for them, therefore, in anything that smacks of censorship, a tension that is not necessarily shared by conservative, would-be censors from the far Right. Because of "Nigger Jim," it is true, some want *Huckleberry Finn* banned from the libraries. But others, who share the same general political outlook and distaste for the nineteenth-century stereotype, feel that the cure of the blue pencil is worse than the disease. And many will resolve, I hope, that the answer is not to consign Mark Twain to oblivion, but to insure that James Baldwin is also on the American Literature reading list. And what this means to me is that censorship from the Left is never likely to mass the concentrated firepower that will come from the other side.

Second, as a result of the 1980 elections, I believe that the "New Right" judges itself to be in the driver's seat in pressing for its objectives, many of which will produce the kind of litigation that Bob O'Neil describes. Whether or not the Moral Majority, or the Christian Voice, or one of the other mutations of that political breed actually played a decisive role in the 1980 elections, or whether more generalized frustrations such as the economy are really the critical force, I think is beside the point. The fact of the matter is that these groups perceive that they played a decisive and critical role. Undoubtedly, they are therefore ready and willing to commit themselves to a much stronger effort in the years ahead.

Third, these groups have not only the motivation and the political will, but also the enormous financial resources, organizational sophistication, and political machinery in place for mounting their challenge—national conservative organizations are reportedly this very moment providing funding, publicity, and technical assistance of various kinds to local groups and organizations who are interested in censoring either textbooks or curriculum. All of this, I think, makes it likely that the 1980s will see repeated, and perhaps better organized, attempts to influence school boards to make "proper" decisions about curricula, texts, library offerings, and the like. And probably these efforts will give rise to numerous court suits and countersuits of the kinds Bob O'Neil has outlined.

The general reluctance of courts, it seems to me, to enter these controversies is certainly due in large measure to their feelings that it is not their function to operate as super school boards and, therefore, except in blatant cases, to defer to local school board judgments and decisions. That understanding, in the absence of countervailing pressure, augurs well, I think, for New Right-inspired censorship and against the significant availability of any widespread judicial remedy.

Fortunately, I would submit that there are a few countervailing pressures. One is the extraordinary sensitivity which the judiciary, the Supreme Court in particular, has shown to the constitutional proscription for separation of church and state. In that area, judicial intervention has not been reluctant. It has been vigilant, even aggressively protective, to date.

It is precisely in that area that the New Right and its strategies of censorship are likely to be most vulnerable. For far from separating church and state issues, the New Right tends to confuse and consciously or unconsciously intertwine them. During the last campaign, I was highly critical of the Moral Majority and similar organizations for taking secular issues and attributing to them a scriptural basis or foundation and a religious aura. My predecesor, Harold Hughes—a devout, born-again Christian himself—is fond of saying he's combed all the books of the Bible and can't find for the life of him where God actually took a position on the merits of the Panama Canal Treaty.

So the New Right does have a political platform; but it is not the New Testament, and the two should not be confused. In the textbook purging and curriculum cleansing efforts that the New Right is backing, the mirror image of their campaign tactics, I think, is descernible. These efforts involve taking religious issues ranging from the theory of creation to personal liberty and morality and assigning responsibility for their inculcation to civil instititutions, our public schools. In those circumstances, I cannot believe that a judicial system which has so assiduously safeguarded the necessary separation of church and state will long remain tolerant of that type of encroachment. In sum then, I believe that the political and social trends of the 1980s are likely to lead to increasing attempts for the politically motivated injection of religion into curricula and library policies and, as a consequence, that the courts may possibly become far more active in this area as well.

THE ROLE OF THE SCHOOLS

Mr. Glasser:

I think the problem in this area, as several of the discussions have pointed out, flows from what the nature of the schools is or should be. Traditionally, First Amendment issues in this country have been played out in public forums of one kind or another in which it has been easy to take the position that the government has no role in the selection or promotion of content and, at best, plays a role of traffic cop and little else. In a case like *Skokie*,[1] that position is strongly taken and content cannot be the basis for the decision; therefore, everybody knows that government's role is just to let a hundred flowers bloom. The trouble in the schools is that there is room on the shelf for only ninety-five flowers and somebody has to decide which five don't get included.

But in the schools, the purpose of the schools is content. It is the legitimate, professional business of the schools to make distinctions based on content. Thus, while content-based decisions are prohibited in public forums, and are therefore subject to any easy, absolute rule for those of us who support the First Amendment, content-based decisions are not only not prohibited, they are required in the schools. To suggest that this should be done in a value-free way, that we should have the schools teach about values but not teach values themselves, is, I think, disingenuous. The schools have always been carriers of values, and it has always been a part of the accepted theory of public schools in this society that that is their function. Their function is to socialize children into the democratic society. That has been part of the rationale that everybody—perhaps without a lot of thought—has accepted.

As the historian Leonard Levy pointed out in his writings about Thomas Jefferson, and as Norman Dorsen repeated, "You are what you read," with respect to your role as a citizen. Jefferson felt so strongly about this that he engaged in some activities at the University of Virginia which most of us would call censorship, because of his fears that the Tories would gain a foothold there and reverse the Revolution. Plato, of course, in discussing the role of education, was much more blunt and basically said that education is in large part indoctrination, that what schools ought to be doing in society is socializing children into the values that the society decides are its own.

We have all implicitly accepted that through the years. The ACLU has talked about how part of the role of schools is to teach the Bill of Rights. And part of the way you teach the Bill of Rights is to act it out. You don't just teach it in social studies classes. You don't just talk about James Madison and free speech. You let the children distribute leaflets and so forth.

But both in the formal curriculum and in the way the school is organized, it has always been accepted by everyone that schools are and should be carriers of values. So when people start talking about racist curriculum and sexist curriculum, they are talking about the schools as carriers of values.

If you look at the differences between the books on the library shelves, and in the literature courses that I took in the fifties in the public schools of New York City and the books that my children read today, what you see is a map of the change in social mores. But in both instances the school was transmitting values. It is true that we read *Ivanhoe* and *Giants of the Earth,* and the miracle was that so many of us survived them. But they were, for certain, transmitting values. Those values were fairly constrained. They reflected a different society; they reflected a society which was much less in flux than the society today. But the schools have always done that. When that happens, there is a problem that traditional analysis of the First Amendment in the public forum does not permit you to deal with in traditional ways.

Usually the question of "who decides" is a forbidden question. The answer is, No one decides. Everybody says what they want and the town council in Skokie, Illinois, or Jackson, Mississippi, doesn't get to decide about whether what they want is a good thing or not. But the question in schools always becomes, Who decides and according to what procedure? There are delegation theories that say it is alright if the librarian does it according to professional standards, but that it is not alright if the school board does it according to politically perceived standards. I don't think that delegation theories help solve the problem, because it still involves making content distinctions that do involve the carrying of values.

We call it censorship only when the procedures and the locus of the decision somehow depart from the routine with which we have all come to feel comfortable. That, in fact, was the majority decision in the *Pico* case.[2] Though the Second Circuit Court of Appeals did as good a job as possible in articulating that point of view, what it amounted to was that in this instance the selection was so crude, so unsubtle, so far from the normal procedures, that it could not be permitted. What that really means is that what is unconstitutional is not the selection of content but a lack of subtlety. As soon as everybody recognizes that, we won't be able to win these cases anymore.

And I'm not sure we won this one. We were unable to persuade a good district court judge that there was even a First Amendment issue involved worthy of scrutiny. We were also unable to persuade at least one of the three judges in the Second Circuit panel, who is normally good on First Amendment issues and on student rights issues, of the same thing. And we barely persuaded one of the two judges who ruled our way that it was enough of an issue to be remanded for trial. The one judge we persuaded all the way was a district judge sitting by designation. That is not what I would call a secure victory, and it came in the context of facts which were as favorable as possible for making out a clear case of censorship. It is very hard to look at the facts of that case and conclude otherwise. And we had that problem because the school board people got up and said, "We represent the community and the community's values are the values which should be reflected in the school. That is our job, and if they don't like it, their remedy is to vote us out of office. . . ."

We don't have any problem when the school functions as a public forum. When somebody wants to dissent from that official selection of values—when a student wants to dissent as in the *Tinker* case,[3] or a teacher wants to dissent as in the *James* case,[4]—the school is a public forum, and traditional public forum analysis applies. But when you are dealing not with dissent from curriculum and content selection but with the official selection itself, you have a whole different set of problems.

Schools did not matter a lot to most people until very recently. They are now a crucial economic institution and that has focused everybody's attention on them. But more than that, they have become a crucial socializing institution in a way that they never were before. Schools and television, and possibly a couple of other institutions, have begun to supplant families and the church as a way of life; they have homogenized values and have become carriers of those values, so that parents are coming to grips with things that they can't control. The reason why haircuts become a problem in the school is because parents can't make their children get one anymore. Therefore they try to transfer that problem to the school, and everything becomes a problem for the school, including sex education. You have to deal with the fact that there are parents who feel that they are losing their ability to transmit values to their children through their family or through their religious institutions. They feel that has been taken out of their hands by these larger institutions which are controlled by people whose values they don't share. That presents a problem in the modern world that never before existed quite to that degree. The contest over values now takes place in an institution controlled by the state. That never happened before. Now the government sponsors education and that becomes the forum in which the transmission of values takes place.

In the past, if you didn't like what went on in the public schools, you withdrew your children from them. Now we are all Amish. Now what is happening is that we are all confronted with how we are going to preserve what we value for our children. The result is a contagion of rights movements that has spread to everybody. Everybody is contesting for their rights. First, it was to dissent from the official policy, but now it is to control the official policy.

The Moral Majority has discovered the First Amendment. And the creationists have discovered the First Amendment. We are all getting hoisted by our own petard and are increasingly going to be hoisted unless we think this thing through.

We have been successful and will continue to be successful only in cases in which our opponents are crude and act in ways that none of us, including the courts, have trouble labeling as censorship. But the real issue of selection of content, of transmission of values, is something that has always gone on. Censorship is really what this problem is about. I am not confident that the problem is resolvable in anything like traditional First Amendment terms. I think it is going to get worse. I think that the curriculum issue, implicit in the whole scientific creation issue—as soon as it becomes even more sophisticated than it is now—is going to present us with a problem which will make *Pico* look like a piece of cake (and we may not even win *Pico*). I think that this larger political-social trend is really what we have to keep in mind as we discuss the particular and narrower litigation strategies and analytic concepts that will occupy the rest of the colloquium.

APPROACHES OF THE NEW RIGHT

Mr. Park:

It is now clear that a coalition has developed among ultra-conservative right-wing organizations in America. The coalition, often call the New Right, has shown considerable success in the use of issue politics. The leadership is relatively young and their grass-roots support systems appear to be rather extensive. The coalition is capable of raising large sums of money and is technologically sophisticated. Within the religious component of the New Right is evidence of interaction among relatively small, but well-organized, groups of Catholics, Fundamentalists, and Mormons. In terms of the history of rightist coalitions, such a phenomenon is perhaps significant. We appear to be witnessing a coalition on the political extreme that will be with us for the forseeable future.

A good deal of social science data suggests that the growth of organizations on the political extreme, both left and right, may be attributed to confusion, and change of society. Given the levels of change and frustration today, we can expect the conditions for the growth of such organizations to continue.

It is interesting to ponder how it is possible to keep folks dancing after the band has played. I speak specifically of how a political coalition such as the New Right can maintain its effectiveness after an election. Perhaps one of the mechanisms for coalition maintenance has surfaced in the context of what is being called the Pro-Family Movement. The Pro-Family Movement is essentially a coalition of organizations within the New and Religious Right, and it appears likely that we will be hearing more from this "movement," especially in the context of social and moral issues.

Three issues appear to be surfacing that may relate to future litigation. The first centers on the definition of religion; or, more specifically, secular humanism or secularism as a state religion. William Ball, a lawyer associated with the Pro-Family Movement, notes that it may be possible to view religion as belief, not body, creed, or cult. His argument, if I understand him correctly, is that if religion in the Constitutional sense can be determined to include theistic as well as nontheistic belief, it would then follow that the doctrine of separation of church and state proscribes government support for religion on the advocacy of particular religious beliefs over others without regard to whether such religion is theistic or nontheistic in nature.

There has been a noticeable increase in the amount of literature distributed to the public by the New Right regarding the issues of secularism and secular humanism as a state religion. It appears likely that future litigation may press the courts to define religion and that we will see a continuation of debate about secularism as "state religion."

A second and somewhat related area of interest is the matter of invasion of privacy. The Hatch Amendment, enacted November 2, 1978 (Public Law 95-561), appears to raise some interesting and perhaps unanticipated controversy. The Hatch Amendment was designed to protect pupil and parental rights and to provide an opportunity for parents to examine educational programs and procedures. While such protections are certainly appropriate, there appear to be some instances in which educators have found it difficult to maintain classroom discussion because of parents and students declaring that they cannot answer questions that *in any way* relate to values, beliefs, judgment, or world view. It seems possible to suggest we may find some organized efforts to press such debates to the point of litigation. Should this occur, what exactly are the limits of invasion of privacy in classroom discussion? And what "exactly" are appropriate "teaching techniques" and "social and psychological techniques" in the classroom? At what point does an invasion of the students' privacy occur? The general area appears to be most problematic and may become an issue of increasing interest.

There is a third, and final point, I would like to explore. I choose to call it the "end-run solution." Perhaps the end-run solution may be described by sharing the remarks of Phyllis Schlafly in the December 1980 issue of *Eagle Forum.* Regarding the legislation for the drafting of women, she writes, "If the U.S. Supreme Court makes the wrong decision in this most important case, we must be ready to move immediately to demand that Congress withdraw jurisdiction from the Federal Courts so that they cannot force our young women into the Army." Given the political skills within the New Right and the social issues on which they have organized, it appears likely we may see an attempt to short-circuit court jurisdiction through the use of political pressure.

Several other items may be noted. The first is a recent fund-raising letter from the Reverend Falwell seeking funds to stop sex education. I would expect that within the next few months we are going to see a good deal of rhetoric about sex education. We may also note the creation of a Stop Textbook-Censorship Committee that has been formed by Phyllis Schlafly to stop what she regards as the radic-lib attempt to remove "pro-family" words from textbooks.

I also call your attention to a rather fascinating bill, actively supported by the New Right, called the Family Protection Act. The original bill (S1808), introduced by Senator Laxalt in the 96th Congress, provides an indication of the direction the New Right would take to change our public schools. The bill deserves a close review by educators and the public.

In the meantime, the phones continue to ring with increasing frequency in the offices of the American Library Association and the National Education Association. Teachers, administrators, and parents are becoming increasingly concerned about the pressure and rhetoric from the New Right.

Ms. Krug:

What is the American Library Association's interest in the whole area of First Amendment concerns, particularly the right to read, the right to speak, and freedom of the press? American librarianship has as one of its foundations the right to acquire for library collections materials representing views across the broad social and political spectra, and to include them in collections; and, conversely, to make this information, these ideas, available to anyone who needs or wants them regardless of age, race, religion, national origin, social and political views, or background. The main problem in that rather broad statement is the word "age." Most of our problems relate to age. Traditionally, censorship has been visited upon, or at least attempted upon, materials for three reasons—namely, explicit sexuality (or just sexuality, period), religious content, and political content. More recently, social content, that is racism, sexism, and so forth, has become a fourth reason. Almost all of our problems revolve around bad language or so-called explicit, sexual descriptions. In many instances, this is merely a smokescreen, but it is an effective smokescreen because the community goes up in arms when it hears, "Your children have access in the library to these kinds of materials. Is this what you want?" I have received innumerable calls recently from people who start out by saying, "I thought libraries were safe. I used to send my kids there on Saturday afternoon." And I say, "No, we are not a babysitting service. Ideas are dangerous and you are just becoming aware of that fact." That is the basic problem—ideas are dangerous, particularly ideas that are broadly representative of social and political thought.

We have had a large increase in activity in the Office for Intellectual Freedom since 4 November 1980. The increase began several months earlier, but literally on November 4, at noon, the place exploded. The Office for Intellectual Freedom is the reporting location for the nation's librarians. We also tend to learn a great deal about pressures being brought to bear on teachers, on broadcasters, on journalists, and on artists. Our incidents increased in the first two weeks after the election, from between three to five times. Now they have begun to decrease, but they are nowhere near our normal pattern for December and January in the past five years. We are substantially above where we were even a year ago in terms of incidents reported. In almost all cases, the people complaining to the librarians and to the teachers have identified themselves as members of, believers in, or supporters of the

Moral Majority or as fundamentalist ministers. You have undoubtedly seen in your newspapers material relating to this increase. It became a story in the *Los Angeles Times* on 12 November 1980 and was picked up by literally hundreds of newspapers across the United States after that.

I am not calling people members of the Moral Majority. *They* have identified themselves as such. I think it is important to realize that people are proud to identify themselves with what is seen as a surging, conservative movement. I refer to the groups on the political spectrum as right of center, left of center, and middle, rather than attaching these labels. But they are proud to be associated with these groups and they are letting us know that they have the whole force of the Moral Majority, which Falwell, at least, claims as being at least sixty to eighty million people, behind them. So, I think we are dealing with a force made all the more serious because of their now much-improved self-image.

At the same time—and I think it is very important to remember this—we are receiving complaints from the left of center. We have recently had complaints against *The Adventures of Huckleberry Finn*; about *The Merchant of Venice*, for its alleged anti-Semitism; about *The Godfather*, the film, for the view that it perpetuates about Italian Americans, and so on. These, at least, are titles we all recognize. So pressures from the left of center continue. Sometimes it becomes very difficult to cope with pressures from the left of center because, as has already been mentioned, many of us feel closer to that political ideology than we do to the ideology propounded by the right of center.

Nevertheless, it is the stand of the American Library Association, and my own personal belief, that censorship is censorship is censorship. When people walk into libraries and schools and attempt to remove from the collection, from the curriculum, those materials containing ideas with which they disagree, that is censorship.

I want to make a few points that will affect future discussion of litigation strategy. First of all, there is a difference between vendors of materials which contain ideas and information—that is, bookstores, newsstands, and so on—and libraries, and, to a lesser extent, schools. I am sure we will eventually get into the finer points of the distinctions in all of these points. However, the distinction, going in, is that bookstores, newsstands, and so on are commercially active organizations. Libraries, particularly, are passive, noncommercial institutions. We used this issue in the case *Moore* v.

Younger,[5] which was the library profession's challenge of the California harmful-matter statute as it applies to the profession. We won on that particular point. We distinguished *Ginsberg v. New York*[6] in order to make our point. So we do have that kind of precedent. Unfortunately, we won at the local level. And we have a decision that has not been reported and, in theory, is binding only on the Los Angeles County court system.

Second, there is a difference between school classrooms and school and public libraries. When children, young people, are in schools, in school classrooms, they are by and large a captive audience. I think an accommodation has to be made for the fact that they are captive. Libraries, on the other hand, provide young people, indeed all people, with the choice to select those materials that they want to read, that they want to involve themselves in. I think that is another important distinction.

Third, there is a distinction between school libraries and public libraries. Interestingly, we have had a substantial increase in the number of attacks on public libraries, which I find far easier to defend against, because in the public library you are dealing with a broad spectrum of the society, not a specific group. However, school libraries have to be looked at carefully, and we can use the point that it is not required for any student to go into any library and select any particular piece of material. Indeed, what we are trying to help them do is develop their ability to think and to come to decisions appropriate for a constitutional republic.

Fourth, I share the concern already expressed by the panelists, and particularly by Bob O'Neil, about self-censorship. But at this point, let's go to the nonacquisition of materials. The problem is that we tell communities that they have to develop guidelines for their own collections based upon the needs of their own constituency. Having done that, it is very difficult to walk in and to say, "What! You don't have Judy Blume in your collection?" Now Judy Blume might be the most popular author among young people today in the range of fourth grade to eighth grade. She has published such things as *Are You There, God? It's Me, Margaret; Blubber; Then Again, Maybe I Won't*, and so on. She also wrote *Wifey*, which is an adult book, and she wrote, *Forever*, which is about the experience of first love, complete with sex outside marriage. The interesting thing about Blume's books is that she doesn't have morals in them. She is talking to the young people in their language and saying that sometimes you are going to do things and there won't be a stigma attached. And that indeed is the crux of the problem with the Judy Blume books, according to the complainers. She is probably the most attacked young person's author today. But it is hard to walk into a library and say, "You don't have Judy Blume." And the staff come back to us and say, "But our community standards and our people aren't going to use Judy Blume because they are not at that point." That is not true, but it's so hard to prove it and to get people to the point where they are open and are going to look at and select the materials that the community really does want. This is the case even if it is an unarticulated need and really should be provided.

Finally, we have a very interesting provision in many of the state obscenity laws and harmful-to-minors statutes. We have what are called exemptions. I call them do-gooder exemptions, and they are basically exemptions for libraries and librarians, museums, schools, and hospitals which say these classes are exempt from the provisions of the law. I have not done anything since April 1976 in terms of compiling the exemptions, so I am giving you outdated information ... although that information has not changed radically over the past five years, it has changed a little. In the general obscenity laws (state statutes), there were six states that had do-gooder exemptions for librarians. We began to work for such exemptions in 1969 because we felt that it was important to protect the ability of librarians to select from the broad spectrum of materials that were available and we felt we had to give them something to stand against. I think it was a wise move in 1969; at this point, I am reconsidering my position. But I have not yet decided to let go of these exemptions which have served us well, although we do have conflicting state decisions. Six state statutes in 1976 did have exemptions for librarians and other do-gooders. In the harmful-to-minors laws or provisions, there were eleven states that exempted librarians. One of the states was Illinois, which did not have a flat-out exemption but did have an affirmative defense written into the harmful-to-minors provision. Because of the Oak Lawn case and Nancy Czerwiec, we have had a bill introduced in the Illinois legislature to amend the Illinois Obscenity Law, specifically and solely to remove the exemption for librarians. Nancy Czerwiec told me, "Once we get this bill through, you can tell your friend, Michael O'Brian [the librarian in Oak Lawn], that we are going to get him." I don't think she is going to get him. *Show Me!* was tried in four cases in three courts in the United

States and one in Canada, and it was exonerated unanimously every time. The book is not obscene. But the pressure that can be brought on librarians can force us to err on the side of caution. When you begin erring on the side of caution, you not only undermine the role that librarians have performed in the constitutional republic for at least the last one hundred years, but you also open yourself to incredible amounts of self-censorship.

These are some of the areas and some of the concerns that we bring to the colloquium. Together, I hope we can find our way to a light at the end of the tunnel.

Anthony Schulte:

Judy, in those states that have exemptions, do the exemptions apply to the library or the librarian? I thought I heard you say it both ways.

Ms. Krug:

It applies to the library, but also to the person. One of our main concerns over the years has been to remove the pressures from the person and place them on the book or material. Let's put the book on trial. Let's not put the public library or the person on trial.

Anthony Schulte:

It applies to the librarian whether it is in a school library or a public library?

Ms. Krug:

The state obscenity statutes or the harmful-to-minors statutes apply to both kinds of institutions.

COMMUNITY CONTROL

Stephen Pevar:

There are so many possible issues that we can discuss. Maybe we can begin by trying to isolate those threshold issues, in which the thread would run through almost every other discussion. One of those is the extent to which a local community can and should regulate its schools. The case that I am handling now, *Fogarty* v. *Atchley*,[7] involves removing a particular book from the classroom (and, by the way, this may be a fifth model because it is not encompassed by the four in Mr. O'Neil's discussion). But the issue there really is the extent to which a community can and should control the schools. Here is a predominantly Mormon community which objects to *One Flew over the Cuckoo's Nest*, not necessarily because of content—you don't have here the pall of orthodoxy problems as in the Second Circuit cases—but they just don't like the use of certain words. It is as much a moral and ethical as a religious viewpoint. The difficulty that I have faced in the case is that I am confronted by very sincere and well-meaning parents and members of the school board, who just don't want their children being exposed to it. They have left the book in the library. A teacher did assign the book, although he assigned it on an optional basis. But they just said, "Let's leave it in the library; if the kids want to read it, fine. But we don't even want a teacher to suggest that this is an appropriate book. Leave that to the parents."

Perhaps the one issue that is most difficult for me personally to confront in this case is the extent to which the community can and should control the public schools.

Henry Kaufman:

I know Steve Arons has written on the subject. Mr Arons?

Stephen Arons:

What you are suggesting is that part of the war we are looking at here is between different elements in the community, some of whom want some books and some of whom want others. One way of rephrasing the question is to ask whether it is possible for the school board to make selections or influence policy about the use of books without somebody stepping on somebody's right to read or other kinds of personal rights. I take it in this case you are defending people who want to have this book discussed in class, mentioned in class, against people who don't. The question only arises because of the majoritarian structure of schooling in the first place.

Henry Kaufman:

Does it make a difference whether or not there is unanimity in the district or if the community is equally divided on the value of a particular book in terms of community rights or obligations?

Stephen Arons:

I would say it does not make a difference. The case does not come up if there is unanimity.

Henry Kaufman:

Maybe people should know the title of your *Harvard Civil Rights Law Review* piece, because it is illuminating to me, if it says what its title suggests—*Manipulation of Consciousness: A First Amendment Critique of Schooling.* I assume you are suggesting schooling, in and of itself, may present First Amendment problems, whoever is in control of the schools.

Stephen Pevar:

I don't think there is any school in the United States that spends more time discussing the Communist Manifesto than the Bill of Rights. Every school makes content choices and everyone who is a product of our public school system has been given a lot more content about certain things and deliberately not exposed at all, or as much, to certain others. So that in my case, the school board said, "Well, we made a mistake; we hired a teacher from the East. Believe me, we will never do it again. Just because of the fortuity [sic] that we had John Fogarty this year and he introduced a certain book into our public schools, what gives him the right? Don't worry, this won't come up again, because when we will hire, our recruitment process will be more severe." It was a real tough case ideologically for me, trying to defend a very unpopular teacher in that school system and trying to defend a book that the community as a whole, I'm convinced, didn't want assigned to any student.

Frank Askin:

Here is a case in point. I was litigating a case in which I was representing high school students who, as part of a drama class, were putting on a play called *Moon Children,* which had many obscenities. Annually the teacher of the drama class, in conjunction with the students but under the teacher's ultimate control and guidance, picked the play. Suddenly, three days before the performance, the principal learned of the play they were putting on and decided that he would have to edit the script. The teacher objected but she couldn't do very much. The principal took the script and returned the edited version to the class, and this was the way the play was to be performed with all of the obscenities removed. And, in fact, in this particular play, the obscenities are integral to the entire mood of the play, the theme. We had expert witnesses to testify to that fact. It went into court and the problem appeared to be, Who could control the content of the class, the students or the principal? It was obviously an unequal contest.

Students don't have the right to decide what they are going to learn in school, what curricular materials are going to be chosen. It is clear that you can't make that argument. How can you say the students are going to control their curriculum? In that confrontation, it was obvious we had to lose if that was going to be the ultimate issue. The issue had to be, To which entity was that authority delegated? And if what we clearly had over a period of time was delegation of the selection of classroom material to the teacher in the classroom, then the issue was *not* whether the students or the principal could choose or the principal through the board of education could control curriculum material. It was a violation of the preexisting process for the principal to suddenly intervene based on some kind of ideological content with which he happened to disagree, or even with which the community or the school board disagreed. In the ultimate analysis, it seemed to me the issue was one of a process as opposed to the content of the material. It was the process which was being violated and this was probably the only way to protect the system. In fact, it is the very pluralism of the educational system which is the only protection and salvation for freedom and against censorship within the schools.

INFORMING VERSUS INDOCTRINATING

William Van Alstyne:

The advice you have just heard basically urges one to take proper advantage of the fact that school boards do typically delegate authority over the selection of school books to others. Accordingly, there is a great deal to be gained in insisting that school boards not presume to disregard the legal process they themselves chose to provide. The point is that in the absence of a proper rescission of such power as the school board has vested in others (such as librarians and teachers), *ad hoc* disregard of the board's own rules, even by the board itself, may be subject to injunctive relief. To the extent that this is so, it may be extremely helpful in dealing with those instances in which school boards tend to move on impulse, that is, simply caving in to some outside political demand that certain books be removed from library or from classroom use.

Nevertheless, useful as this advice is, I think it cannot be sufficient. The advice concedes (as it must) that such delegation of authority respecting curricular detail, book selection, classroom assignments, and so forth as may be made by regulation or by statute can, of course, be retracted by the same power that provided that delegation. Accordingly, the argument concedes that *if* community sentiment for "censorship" is sufficiently strong and persistent, it can have its way. Thus, the quick victory one may achieve in a given case (by proving that the school board has acted in derogation of power it has delegated to others) may subsequently be overwhelmed insofar as the board thereafter, consistent with state law, withdraws the delegation and vests in itself the discretion to make such decisions. By implication, the board may indeed, without interference from the Constitution of the United States, use tax-supported compulsory public education to propagandize captive classes of students according to prevailing majoritarian preferences, with an enforceable resolve to keep from our classroom and school libraries whatever material they dislike. Respectfully, I do not share that view of the matter or that view of the futility of the Constitution in respect to academic freedom.

The American Heritage Dictionary reports that to educate is "to inform, from a middle English word, from a Latin word, to bring up. To bring up by informing." There, I suggest to you, is an intelligent point of departure. To bring up by informing is in contradistinction to bringing up by inculcating, by proselytizing, by indoctrinating.

Also there is some positive law adjudicated by the Supreme Court that at least provides a touch point of comparison for the distinction between the two which will always be somewhat elusive and understandably subject to disagreements among intelligent people. The distinction is reflected, interestingly enough, in the Court's own adjudication of some of the establishment clause qualifications.

The Court is always careful, having held a particular practice in the public school to be in violation of the establishment clause, swiftly to add that this, of course, does not preclude the school from *informing* students with respect to religion, from introducing them to it, from showing them comparative uses of it and so on. And examples are given in a contrasting technique to "inform" and to "indoctrinate"; the latter is forbidden by the establishment clause. As I say, the boundary line is elusive, but although twilight is sometimes difficult to identify, nighttime is plain enough.

Some persons are in a position to monitor "nighttime." In my view, the instructor is in a position and has suitable standing to do so because of academic freedom. The instructor stands astride the gulf between the parents and students, taxpayers and the school board, at least to rebel against a kind of directive which is unmistakably a directive to inculcate, to indoctrinate, to proselytize, systematically to examine only a certain perspective, for instance, of the American novel or capitalism. So a school board plan to "teach" the virtue of the Bill of Rights solely by a regimen of prescribed and partisan indoctrination, to the exclusion of rival views, should be classically inimical to this society as I think that it is also forbidden by the First Amendment.

Some effort must be made to distinguish between bringing up by informing and rendering an individual safe by a process of indoctrination. The technique of indoctrination is quite clear to the extent that it is systematically expounded by the prevailing majority. This is an improper—that is to say anti-First Amendment—compulsory tax use of governmentally operated, public education.

The remaining problem is merely the practical one, that of finding suitable parties, and the infinitely difficult, but still merely practical one, of fashioning the evidence in order to convince a judge. But I do take fundamental exception to the concession that because public schools have historically—in almost pre-First Amendment, doctrinal times—presumed to reflect an entrenched ideology of a local majority, it therefore follows that a *constitutional* propriety for such practices has already been established. This would be a disastrous syllogism for this group to accept.

POLITICAL STRATEGIES

Henry Kaufman:

I would like at least to air the problem of possible legislation in an area such as the Family Protection Act, or the question of whether we could face in this current political climate an effort to cut off federal court jurisdiction to enforce First Amendment rights. Senator Culver, do you think what we are dealing with is such a powerful force that it could literally undermine and undo some of the basic premises we have had in regard to the judicial vindication of First Amendment rights?

Mr. Culver:

Actually, I think there is this inherent fragility that was just referred to, and the point is extremely valid that what is necessary to sustain and maintain this whole framework is a general public consensus. I am not that familiar with the

Laxalt bill and the Family Protection Act. But clearly in the absence of a countervailing public expression of a contrary view—given the nature of our political process and system—democracy and the values we represent and care about greatly are not self-renewing. There is nothing automatic about them. We all know that even the Supreme Court follows the election returns. We have seen the powers of appointment to that body and there is certainly nothing in cement in any of these areas. One of the powerful forces the Far Right is benefiting from is the exploitation and the apathy of the majority. To the extent to which they, relatively speaking, go out and do a better job of targeting and effectively marshalling and mobilizing public opinion totally within the bounds of the political process, they're going to be successful.

William Van Alstyne:

Let me ask what seems to me to be a corollary question: Should we necessarily assume, with regard to some of these fundamental premises, such as the First Amendment and the basic purposes of education, that there is a political Right that will rally around the opposite point of view? Or isn't it even possible that the civil liberties point of view will attract more than just what we typically broadly call the Right or the Left?

Dr. Glasser:

I think what is happening is that the people whom we perceive to be on the other side of this issue are making their arguments precisely in terms such as Bill Van Alstyne just described. They are not talking any longer of excluding anything; they are talking about things like equal-time provisions and including things. And in the creationist business, for example, you do get involved very much in the questions, What is Religion?, What is science?, and What is appropriate to teach in a biology class? In those discussions, the distinction between indoctrination and informing, indoctrination and education, are much less easy to discern than a discussion around this table would suggest. Of course, the obvious answer to the contextual problem I posed is what Bill suggested. I mean, the only thing we can do is attempt to preserve the distinction between indoctrination and information, between indoctrination and education.

The twilight that Bill referred to is much broader than the real twilight, which passes in an instant from day to night and which gets us into the position where we can't say exactly when that instant is, but we know that night has arrived. In

the schools, it's all twilight. And the distinction between education and indoctrination is a harder distinction to maintain
in the places where curriculum is developed and in the actual
classroom than it is in the law reviews. The problem with
litigating these cases is that much of what actually goes on in
public schools could not survive that distinction. I'm talking
about the way in which physics, chemistry, biology, and mathematics are taught. Children are taught by rote. If you ask
most children why you can't divide by zero, their response
will be that the teacher forbids it. They memorized the rule,
and they learned that that's what success is about. There is
a problem in dealing with highly ideological and value-laden
content—and that can infect science classes as well, as the
creationist/evolution controversy shows. The precise problem that I think this colloquium ought to discuss is not whether
to preserve the distinction Bill suggests—that is obviously
what we should do—but how to do it in light of what goes on
in most classrooms and the way in which most things are
actually taught. Good teaching is education, but most teaching is indoctrination. So although one can analytically define
a distinction between indoctrination and education, such a
legal distinction may have less utility in terms of what actually
goes on in the schools.

The creationists have tried to exploit this situation by
claiming that there is scientific evidence to support the biblical account of Genesis and that evolution is being taught as
doctrine. Therefore, they argue, teaching Genesis in biology
classes is no different from teaching different scientific theories of the origins of the cosmos. Of course, there is no scientific
evidence for supernatural creation, and the biblical account
of Genesis is not quite what astronomers who subscribe to the
big-bang theory mean by the big-bang theory. But the creationists have become more subtle. Legislation has evolved (no
pun intended) from flat-out requirements to teach Genesis to
increasingly subtle and sophisticated laws that seem to do
nothing more than say, "All scientific theories should compete." This approach has proven much more difficult to challenge. The distinction between education and indoctrination
is intentionally blurred. For example, at a school board meeting in a little town in Nebraska the right-to-lifers are not
contesting sex education in the schools, but they are seeking
to put in a right-to-life curriculum that carries forward their
political values. In such a case it gets very difficult to maintain
that distinction.

The problem I am suggesting is that what most people

are about is controlling the schools. They want them to be value-carrying institutions. For us to try to preserve the distinction between education and indoctrination is the right course, but one which I think will be increasingly difficult to maintain. It will confine us to a narrower set of issues so that while we litigate in increasingly narrow factual circumstances, the central problem of majoritarian schools will remain. People who have looked at the schools from an educational and political point of view and not from a First Amendment legal point of view, seem much more thoughtful on this question.

Ms. Krug:

When we're dealing with the issues, we have to look at reality, at what the world is now. The Right, particularly, has more money than we can comprehend. It is highly sophisticated; its materials are becoming more sophisticated. It is really moving around some of our major objections, which made excellent litigation points just two or three years ago. We can't give up what we already have; but we have to find new ways to approach them, because judges are only human and have not been capped by God, despite Phyllis Schlafly and the Gablers saying, "We have to pray that the U.S. Supreme Court is going to see the light. We have to pray that the circuit courts are going to see the light." Well, don't pray. Spend that time looking at what reality is and then take the issues that we're concerned with and work them into reality.

JUDICIAL PROSPECTS

Mr. O'Neil:

I'd like to pick up on two earlier comments of two of my on-the-panel colleagues, toward what may be a little more hopeful view of the role of the courts. The first is John Culver's very apt observation that the reluctance that the courts display in other aspects does not extend to what are classically or even recognizably church/state issues. The other is Chuck Park's comment that the definition of religion will be an increasingly fruitful point of departure and may have some as yet unfulfilled potential. I am thinking in terms of several things that have happened, which I find relatively hopeful in this respect. One, of course, is the West Clark biology textbook case.[8] Though not widely publicized, and unreported, and having no application outside Marion County, Indiana, and I think unappealed because it was assumed that it was wiser for the state textbook commission to cut its losses at the superior court level since it would almost certainly be affirmed, it does represent a very striking example of removing from the approved list a textbook whose creationist bias is really more evident in the teacher's manual than it is in the book itself. The whole process that the superior court judge went through is a fascinating analysis that gives me considerable hope. Second, I would point to the district court's and the Third Circuit's analysis in the New Jersey "Transcendental Meditation" case.[9] This is an exceedingly difficult case on the definition of religion, important but largely neglected in terms of the implications it may have for equal-time creationist intrusion into other courses.

Third, I point to the Chattanooga litigation. Professor Le Clerc, I'm sure, knows about the third of the Wiley cases,[10] the most important of the three, really, going into the curriculum and finding a comparative religion course which seemed innocuous on the surface. It looked exactly like the kind of so-called study of religion, which in Schempp[11] and Murray[12] the Supreme Court said was appropriate, indeed in some ways desirable. Yet the further the Court got into it, the clearer it became that this was really back to our proselytizing and, in the end, it was enjoined. So, without disagreeing with anything that has been said about the role of the schools in other areas, I would like to offer a slightly more hopeful observation. I think the curricular modification or the course elimination issue was properly decided in deference to the authority, or, as some would say, the locus of authority in the decisionmaking process. I gather Fogarty has not yet come to a decision, but if that court recognizes, as the district court did in Cary,[13] the distinction between throwing out the course and throwing out the teacher, if you will, I think that distinction will obtain.

That leads finally to an observation about the delegation issue. It goes back to the time I was chairman of the Academic Senate Committee on Academic Freedom at Berkeley, and we had what some will recall as the "Cleaver course" case.[14] The Board of Regents had delegated to the Committee on Courses of each of the divisions, that is to say campuses, the authority to approve courses. In the Cleaver course case, that authority was withdrawn not only for the purpose of disapproving specifically the Cleaver course, but also, in more troublesome degree, for the purpose of disapproving giving credit to the students who were refugees from the canceled

Cleaver course through an "X" course, which had a seemingly open-ended coverage. When the governing board reached that far down, we argued that this was a clear violation of any principle of delegation. Bear in mind that this is higher education, not elementary and secondary. And as many of you recall, we got absolutely nowhere in the California courts. Ever since then, I've been somewhat more pessimistic than I think Professor Yudof and others may be on the delegation issue.

Kenneth Norwick:

There is another aspect to the delegation problem that concerns me. In New York City the mayor has power to appoint certain judges, including criminal court judges. He has now announced that he is going to interrogate prospective judges to see if they agree with him, at least implicitly, on how they should be judges and what policies they should have. By the same analysis, it seems to me, those who appoint and select the librarians or the teachers may well find themselves interrogating prospective appointees for political and ideological points of view; and we may find that we don't have any more book cases because the people to whom the decisions are delegated will be preselected; and the censorship, if that's what it is, will be in the process of selecting the people who will be making those decisions. I would like to hear at some point some analysis of how you litigate the interrogation of prospective librarians.

THE CULTURAL CONTEXT

Stephen Arons:

I take it that our general discussion concerns the political, social, and cultural context in which the technical, legal problems arise. I want to add to that, having spent a fair amount of time talking to people who are involved in these kinds of censorship controversies.

Censorship of books and curriculum is the tip of the iceberg, and it really extends very far down not only to the selection of teachers or the interrogation of teachers and manipulation of job security, but also to things like standardized testing. If you look at history texts, for example, you see all of this. So, even if we are able to cling to some of the distinctions that are being suggested as usable for textbook business, we are going to find that the underlying social force that we are dealing with is not going to go away.

People are discovering that their cultural assumptions are dysfunctional and they are acting it out by taking these traditional, oppressive tactics to achieve the satisfaction of order at any cost. So I think the question for us really is, At a time of cultural confusion, when people are willing to use oppressive tactics, what is the best structure for schooling and the best defense of that structure designed to maintain some kind of pluralism based on that confusion? We look back historically to the twenties, which are not completely identical to the present, but were at least noted for persecution of people to the left and various forms of oppression we are now beginning to look at. You see in the school context that the courts were in part willing to deal with the problem of using schools as indoctrinating institutions for the interests of right-wing politics by securing what has come to be called the right to attend something other than a public school. Now that right doesn't seem to satisfy any of us here, partly for economic reasons, and it applies only to a small number of people.

It is very interesting that if you talk to the teachers or the librarians involved in these censorship struggles, to a person, almost, they have offered compromises. They have said, "Well, I'll only make the book available to those kids who bring a letter from their parents saying it's okay to read it," or "All right, you don't want to read *The Bell Jar*; I'll only teach *The Bell Jar* to the kids whose parents want them to read that, and we'll read *Little Women* with the other kids." And these compromises have been uniformly rejected by political interests.

Ms. Krug:

The political compromises are accepted in some instances. The problem goes back to what Ken was saying, that the people who are willing to stand up are the ones who are generally sure of themselves, have a good professional background, and so on. We can lose those kinds of people easily in many ways, and many of the ways are very underhanded—you never have anything tangible. Rarely do people come out and say, "You're fired." Occasionally they do, but usually they say, "You're fired because. . . ." Very subtle. How do you find a handle to hold on to? If these people are replaced, then what do you have? It goes back to the selection procedure. You're supposed to tell a community, or tell John Fogarty's old school board that they have to bring in somebody else from the streets?

Stephen Arons:

> The only point I'm trying to make is that the impetus behind the people who are interested in censorship often prevents them from accepting the kinds of compromises offered by teachers and librarians.

THE BOOK SELECTION PROCESS

Henry Kaufman:

> Michelle Kamhi has a few things to say to us. She is research assistant and consultant for a project that has been developed by the American Library Association, the Association of American Publishers, and the Association for Supervision and Curriculum Development, among others. The project is to study in an empirical and more systematic way the nature of book selection processes and the incidence of what we might define as censorship actions.

Michelle Kamhi:

> We worked with an advisory group of educators, librarians, and book publishers to develop a very comprehensive survey instrument. The title is "Book and Materials Selection for School Libraries and Classrooms: Procedures, Challenges and Responses." We believe that this will be the most extensive survey of its kind.
>
> Because we feel we have a good deal of very vital information that we want to release in a way that will achieve the maximum impact, I am going to be very limited in what I tell you before the report is published. Of the people who did report challenges, more than a fourth of them said that the rate of challenges in the two-year period beginning 1 September 1978, which was the arbitrary cutoff that we had given them, was higher than the preceding two-year period. And, of course, we heard from Judy Krug that if we were to circulate this questionnaire now, it would be very likely that the reponse to that question would be even higher. About half of the respondents said the challenges were about the same; fewer than ten percent said they were lower.

Henry Kaufman:

> How did you define "challenges?"

Michelle Kamhi:

That was a problem. We wanted to avoid the term "censorship." We used it nowhere in the instrument, because we felt it would be waving a red flag. It was clear from the responses that the interpretations of challenges were different. I think many people read challenges as a very formal and major kind of registering of complaint. Other surveys done on censorship used the term "objections," which would probably give a fuller report on incidents in that respect. So the overall rate that we got was probably lower than the actual experience in the field. Twenty percent of the administrators said that they had some kind of challenges to materials, either library or classroom materials, in the two-year period. Thirty percent of the librarians said that they had such experience. There were a number of factors that indicate that these figures were lower than the actual rate.

The kinds of materials challenged on the local level are the same kinds of things which have been challenged all along. Issues relating to sex and sexuality and also obscenity and profanity in language were among the most frequently cited objections. The kinds of materials challenged were preeminently (this is again on the local level now) library materials, supplementary classroom materials, and, in third place, textbooks. Overall the leading challenged category, both in library and supplementary classroom materials, was contemporary fiction. Those of you dealing with cases know the kinds of things that people are concerned about.

Who initiated the challenge? On the local level, slightly less than eighty percent of the challenges were raised by individuals. Of this number, more than one half involved parents, acting on their own behalf rather than representing any group. They were very much individual situations. The remainder of the challenges were instituted by teachers, community members, school boards, administrators, and so forth.

The state-level situation contrasted very strongly with this. The challenges were far more organized. If not ostensibly, at least there was group action behind the individual challenger, judging from the interviews that I did with the state-level representatives. The kinds of materials that were being challenged on the state level also were quite different.

One crucial question that we asked on the questionnaire was, "Did the challenger attempt to expand or to limit the information and viewpoints in the materials that were available to the students?" On the local level, the response was overwhelmingly to limit. On the state level, however—and I think this gets at the whole question of the sophistication of the groups who are attempting to alter the materials that are in the schools—there was a slightly greater number (about fifty percent) on the side of expanding materials rather than limiting them.

We asked whether there was any form of prior censorship. Was the material, the challenged material, altered or removed *prior to* a formal review? And on the local level in fifty percent of the specific incidents that respondents reported on, there was some form of censorship prior to a formal review of the situation. We did regional breakdowns on the questions, and the incidence of censorship prior to formal review was about seventy percent in the South. This is the final disposition of the case after some kind of formal review: In a third of the cases the challenge was overruled, and in about ten percent of the cases an alternate assignment was offered at the parents' request. I group those together as non-censorship solutions. So you come up with a balance of over fifty percent indicating some degree of censorship. In twenty percent of the cases, there was removal of the material from the school. In other cases, it was a question of limiting access in the library by closed shelving or by requiring parental permission or something of that nature. Some of the most interesting things to look at are the responses on the state level. As I mentioned, the challenges on the state level were far more organized than those on the local level. They were related more to textbooks and thereby to curriculum. Usually, objections related to the entire spectrum of titles under consideration for adoption rather than to any single title, whereas on the local level single books were specified and were the object of challenges. On the state level, more often the attempt was to insert new information or viewpoints into the material.

Most interesting is that in about two-thirds of the cases that were cited on the state level, some degree of outside influence was cited in terms of organized groups. By outside influence I mean groups from outside of the state. Half of all of the respondents on the state level noted the influence of the Gablers. Even more alarming than that, perhaps, all of those on the state level who said that the recent rate of challenges was higher than the rate in the previous two-year period attributed it to the activities of the Gablers and other New Right groups.

One state-level official said that he flatly refused to send any materials to the Gablers. They often requested schedules of hearings and wanted to know what the adoption articles were. He said that he thought it was entirely inappropriate for him to send that kind of information to a group outside the state. Any citizen of his state would be free to receive such information, and although he knew that it would be easy enough for them to obtain it, he felt it was an important distinction to make. Another respondent indicated, "Well, I knew they could get it anyway, so I sent it to them," without really recognizing that there was a very important principle involved there.

We hope that the full report of the study will be released in July 1981.

Anthony Schulte:

Michelle, I want to thank you for making such a discreet presentation, so that we don't have to declare this gathering equivalent to a troopship in time of war.

SCIENTIFIC CREATIONISM

Henry Kaufman:

Dr. Wayne Moyer, executive director of the National Association of Biology Teachers, has offered to give us some information on the work of his group, particularly with regard to the problem of so-called "scientific creationism."

Wayne Moyer:

The people proposing that scientific creationism be put into the public schools in the science curriculum are usually arguing that science itself is a type of religion. They are attempting to formulate for their own purposes the distinction between science and religion. I think the field of epistemology is useful in examining this question. Here we can define three separate fields of knowledge. The first is empirical knowledge which we can obtain through the senses of smell, taste, and so on. Second is the field of revealed knowledge, revealed from on high or by dogmatic belief—for example, astrology, with its belief that the stars guide us, would be revealed knowledge, as would be a belief that the word of God is expressed in the Bible without error. A third area is logical knowledge as we encounter in mathematics.

The problem comes when an attempt is made to use truths that are accepted in one realm to explain observations in another realm, as the creationist proponents are attempting to do. Each realm is exclusive within itself. To underline this distinction, take the wafer used in many Christian communions. To some Christians, that wafer, upon consecration, becomes the body of Christ and is accepted that way by the communicants. Now, if this revealed knowledge is applied to the empirical world and it is said that the wafer is literally the body of Christ, then we can subject it to scientific evaluation. A biochemist looking at the wafer before and after consecration will find no difference whatsoever. If this parallel is kept, that revealed knowledge can be used to interpret empirical knowledge, then we must either accept one or the other and immediately a dilemma is set up. It is only avoided if we keep the two realms of knowledge exclusive within their own realm.

It is entirely proper to use these as supplemental views of the universe. The Bible, the Old Testament in particular, has a number of stories regarding creation, such as the flood and the origin of language at the Tower of Babel. This can be viewed, then, as one set of knowledge within the realm of revealed knowledge. But as soon as it is applied to empirical data, then the student, the public, is forced to choose between either belief in God or the empirical explanation. And that is the dilemma that the creationists are attempting to present. These are supplemental views, in our estimation, of the universe. And we would therefore argue that science should be established by the scientific community. The creationists argue that they have as good a scientific explanation of the origins of man as others; therefore, they propose that it be taught as science. But it is in the realm of revealed truth; one must resort ultimately, then, to belief in God in order to accept their explanation.

We would defend strongly the belief that science, all content of science courses, must pass the test of science and be accepted by the scientific community. However, we also accept that there are alternative ways of viewing the universe and that these sometimes appear to be in conflict with scientific findings. The two are supplemental and we would have no trouble with science teachers looking at creationism as a problem growing out of scientific knowledge but which, of itself, is not science. In the same manner, for example, the moral issues growing out of our knowledge of amniocentesis, cell culture, and chromosome identification, lead to serious moral questions and problems for people, especially a couple who are parenting a potential Down's syndrome child.

Our viewpoint is that scientific creationism is not science, can never be science, because of its very nature. We believe that the creationists are in fact attempting to construct an entire structure of pseudoscience in order to support their belief in the inerrancy of the Bible. It is being proposed in bills that have been introduced in various states. It appeared in almost similar form in Illinois, New York, Florida, and several other states last session and will likely appear in Nebraska this session.

Michelle Kamhi:

I would like to ask Dr. Moyer how his organization is handling the argument of creationists that they have reputable scientists in the scientific community that are presenting their point of view.

Wayne Moyer:

One of the arguments is that a scientist is trained in a particular area and once he gets out of his area he generally gets in hot water when he makes pronouncements. I would not think about making pronouncements about geological knowledge. I would be out of my realm. But that doesn't stop a fundamentalist or an evangelical Christian who has accepted the truth of the Bible. He feels that he has the right to make pronouncements outside of his field. And, in effect, he has violated one of the hallmarks of science, which is to keep an open mind, to accept evidence and to evaluate it as it comes in, against currently held theories. Every theory in science is never proven. It is always being evaluated as new findings are brought in and held up against this theory for examination. None of our theories are ever going to be completely accurate. Even the old idea that the planets go around the earth and the sun goes around the earth worked for a while until new evidence came in and then it no longer worked. It had to be let go when the idea that the sun is the center of our particular planetary system took hold. Even that was replaced in part by the Einsteinian concept of relativity, and, even there, additional modifications will be coming along as new evidence is brought in, so that theory is never proven. Yet the creationist would say that it is proven once and for all, by way of his belief that God made the universe. So in that area he is not entirely talking as a scientist.

Michael Bamberger:

I would disagree that we need not be significantly concerned about challenges from other than the radical Right. I think that one of the things that we have seen in certain areas, with the growth of "single-issue" groups, is that their views and practices are partially modeled upon certain other radical Right groups. They believe that their issue predominates over all other constitutional issues. We see it very clearly, for example, from the feminist group Women Against Pornography, who have said that that issue, the gender discrimination issue, is so vital to our civilization that certain nonobscene, First Amendment protected material must be banned. So I think that we should not mold our mental outlook solely to the Right. The basic right-left dichotomy, or conservative-liberal dichotomy, really is no longer quite as apposite, particularly when you are dealing with single-issue groups.

Michelle Kamhi:

By and large, publishers of textbooks have already responded to these objections, and the materials now coming up for adoption are sensitive to those issues. The issues that predominate in current challenges are the issues of the conservatives, the New Right, creationists, and so forth.

SECOND GENERAL SESSION

The State as Editor or Censor: Book Selection and the Public Schools

Mark G. Yudof

Over the last ten years there have probably been more constitutional challenges to public school library and textbook decisions than in the previous one hundred years. I suspect that there are many reasons for this increase. Resolution of disputes in the public schools is increasingly dominated by rules and formal procedures and legislation and lawsuits, and it is natural that the legalization apparent with regard to collective bargaining, student records, desegregation, treatment of the handicapped, and the like, should spill over into the textbook area. Public opinion polls also show a declining confidence in professionals and public officials, and many are perhaps less accepting of decisions made by experts or elected school representatives. This is particularly true if one is a member of a minority group which feels that the majority's curriculum, textbook, and other school decisions do not reflect its preferences. And with the decline in the view that public schools are above politics, the dissension in values that pervades so many areas—for example, in the role of women—may result in an increased willingness of the losers in the political process to do battle in the courts. This is particularly evident in the movement to dismantle whatever barriers have "separated government from personal morality and religion."[1] As the Public Agenda Foundation put it in a recent study,

> This mode of thinking can be seen . . . in increasing demands for "reviews" of school textbooks. Many Americans have come to feel that the state cannot be neutral to questions of lifestyle; they believe that the forces of government should be harnessed to bring the country back to a particular moral and religious standard.[2]

Textbook controversies arise in many settings. School officials assert their wisdom in educating the young.[3] Elected officials often perceive of themselves as the conduits for transporting the community's values into the schools. Writers, editors, and publishers are gravely concerned with their freedom of expression, and they fear government efforts to eliminate particular ideas and perspectives from school classrooms. Parents have an interest in directing the upbringing of their children and in inculcating particular secular and nonsecular values.[4] Teachers and librarians assert rights to academic freedom, particularly the right to be reasonably autonomous in carrying out their professional responsibilities.[5] Students may assert a right to know, to read, to learn, or to acquire information, or a right not to be subjected to materials they find fundamentally objectionable.[6] And some, including myself, fear government expression itself; for government may take advantage of the captive and immature audience in public schools to indoctrinate children to values that enhance the *status quo*, to undermine their ability in the future to act as "self-controlled" citizens[7] expressing preferences about political, economic, and social questions.[8] The government's capacity to shape beliefs and attitudes may be as destructive of democratic values as direct censorship.[9] And government may accomplish this by picking and choosing among private communicators, by subsidizing the voices of the uncritical, and by denying subsidies to strong and critical voices. Book selection for public school students is an excellent example of a policy arena in which such dangers lurk. But for all its importance, judicial decisions remind one of the ancient Latin motto "Crescit occulto velut arbor aevo" (which loosely translated means "Nothing great has great beginnings"). Courts have reacted tentatively, inconsistently, and sometimes incoherently, notwithstanding (or perhaps because of) the delicate and important nature of the problem. I am reminded of the nineteenth-century reactionary Joseph De Maistre, who admonished that the pure of heart and righteous do not need books; precepts are "imprinted by grace in our hearts." It is only because of our sinful ways that "books and laws became necessary."[10]

Perhaps it is best to begin with the notion that indoctrination is much of what schools are about. But it is not all that schools are about. If government is to educate children, to operate public schools, and to select teachers, books, and courses, a basic decision has been made about the communication of skills, attitudes, values, and beliefs between generations. Education and indoctrination, information and values, cannot be neatly disentangled. Education, after all, is often a process of persuasion. As Elliot Aronson has remarked, one man's propaganda is another's truth.[11] More importantly, socialization and education are not only inextricably linked, but the failure of the adult generation, through the polity, to bring the young into the larger political, economic, and social culture would have disastrous consequences. We have no reason to think that children are inherently good or democratic or tolerant or peaceful. We have even less reason to believe that they are capable of inventing, on their own and without the benefit of the community's experiences, gasoline engines, theories of relativity, and neurosurgical techniques. The dominant languages, modes of computation, and the specific customs and history of the people will and should be taught. And this learning is not value neutral.

The problem, however, lies in devising educational systems that prepare children for adult life without simultaneously sacrificing their ability to reflect upon the ends for which they are being prepared, without indoctrinating them to unbridled allegiance to the *status quo* or to the rightness of current institutional arrangements. Basic knowledge should be communicated while attempting, as best we can, to give the young "ample opportunity of making the decisions upon which these principles are based, and by which they are modified, improved, adapted to changed circumstances or even abandoned if they become entirely unsuited to the new environment."[12] Education can expand the mind and imagination or contract them.[13] The child who is taught nothing of his or her country's cultural, political, and intellectual heritage must be pitied as much as the child who is compelled to conform in all respects to the conventional wisdom. As Ruth Benedict put it, "No civilization has in it any element which in the last analysis is not the contribution of an individual."[14] Yet, individuality does not exist in a vacuum; it is defined by the background of the community.[15]

The inevitable question then is, Who determines what is to be taught in public schools, who does the necessary balancing? The answer, by and large, is that elected representatives, school board members, and school administrators make the choices and are, at least in theory, accountable to the citizenry for their performance. There is no necessary reason why affairs have to be arranged this way; many have proposed alternatives which would enhance, for example, the power of families to make educational choices.[16] But these are our existing legal and institutional arrangements. As the Seventh Circuit recently stated in *Zykan v. Warsaw Community School Corporation,*

> [Public schools have a] broad formative role . . . [which encompasses] the encouragement and nurturing of those fundamental social, political, and moral values that will permit a student to take his place in the community. . . . As a result, the community has a legitimate, even a vital and compelling interest in "the choice [of] and adherence to a suitable curriculum for the benefit of our young citizens. . . ."

> Educational decisions necessarily involve choices regarding what students should read and hear, and particularly in light of the formative purpose of secondary school education, local discretion thus means the freedom to form an opinion regarding the instructional content that will best transmit the basic values of the community.[17]

This necessarily puts the state in the business of editing the curriculum, including making selections of books for inclusion in the school library and for optional or required reading in designated courses. If no such authority existed, if disgruntled parents and others had a "right" to equal time to reply to the state's program, if public schools were public forums in the fullest sense of the phrase (like parks, for example), the educational mission of the schools, including acculturation, would become impossible. As a general matter, despite some wishful thinking to the contrary,[18] schools are not subject to the various balancing of the message doctrines including fairness, a right to reply, equal time, and the like.[19] As Professor (now Judge) Canby has stated,

> "[E]diting is what editors are for; and editing is selection and choice of material." To forbid the managers of ... [public communication] enterprises to select material for inclusion and, necessarily, exclusion would for all practical purposes destroy these endeavors.[20]

If we pause a moment to reflect on these matters, it becomes clear why curricular and book purchasing decisions generally should be left to the state under current institutional arrangements. It simply cannot be the case that because government owns and operates an enterprise devoted to communication it cannot, in good faith, carry out its editorial functions.[21] Where time and resources are scarce, selectivity is inherent in communication. A person does not have a constitutional right to publish his or her article in the law review of a state university, for that undermines the mission of publishing high quality, scholarly articles.[22] Nor should prison rehabilitation programs, state-sponsored psychiatric programs for the mentally infirm, or, for that matter, the President's State of the Union Address be subject to dilution by requirements of fairness, balance, or rights of reply as a matter of constitutional law. Of course such standards sometimes have been voluntarily adopted by statute or regulation or practice for government communications. But if one concedes that public schooling, prison rehabilitation programs, military training, and other government communication efforts are legitimate and, indeed, essential for well-being, then government cannot be denied the editorial power which is the wherewithal to accomplish its objectives. And this logic is bolstered by the fact that school children are a captive audience, an audience captured for the purpose of accomplishing particular educational objectives. They are in school because, through democratic processes, the people have decided they should be there, and hence the duly elected representatives of the people should make the basic editorial decisions. The loss of liberty to parents and children is difficult to justify if the students are a captive audience to private communicators with their own educational or indoctrinational agenda.[23] As Professor Shiffrin succinctly writes,

> To make education compulsory was itself to challenge liberal ideology.
>
> The essence of compulsory education is that the state and not parents will ultimately decide what is best for children.[24]

This is not to say that there are not situations in which the editorial functions of the state may not be limited. There are constitutional doctrines of limitation, and I will soon elaborate on them. Nor is it to say that persons should not have access to schools for communication purposes,[25] or that students do not have First Amendment rights of communication which they take with them to public schools.[26] But the standard is one of nondisruption or compatibility of the educational process, the mission of the schools, and private expression.[27] My point is that the loss of the power to choose and select textbooks and courses is inherently incompatible with the schooling enterprise. For this reason, and many of you may disagree, I do not know how the various derivative First Amendment rights entitled rights to know, to learn, or to acquire information can be given much credence in the public school setting.[28] In my view the "right to know," as articulated by the Supreme Court,[29] is no more than artistic camouflage to protect the interest of a willing speaker who seeks to communicate with a willing listener.[30] If students have a right to know, then they should have a constitutional right to demand courses in public schools that are not offered for financial or other reasons. Any question in a class, as a constitutional matter, would require an answer—no matter that the question relates to the French Revolution and is asked in an algebra class or that every other student in the class has no desire to acquire such information at that time and place. Students, presumably, would be entitled to choose their own books at government expense. And no librarian could refuse to purchase a book sought by a student. In other spheres, public libraries devoted to particular subjects, say the social sciences, would fall under the constitutional axe if nineteenth-century Russian novels were requested. Museum collections would quickly follow. There simply is no limiting principle, apart from the question of the uncertain constitutional pedigree of such a right. This is a far cry from situations where a lawyer or pharmacist wishes to communicate information about his or her services and products to the public, where many consumers of the services and products wish to acquire the information, and where government forbids the willing parties from communicating with each other by particular means.

If students and parents cannot edit the curriculum and choose books for themselves in the guise of a right to know, surely authors, editors, and publishers have no constitutional right to have their books purchased by the state for dissemination in public schools. To my knowledge, no court has arrived at such a holding.[31] This would effectively place the power to edit the curriculum in the hands of private, disinterested parties—neither parents nor the state—and they would have an audience captured for them by governmental coercion. Further, it is one thing for government to censor books and limit their distribution, and quite another to require the state to purchase books in the name of the First Amendment rights of its producers. Surely such absolutists as Justices Black and Douglas, who did not believe that federal and state governments had any authority to ban books on obscenity, national security, or other grounds would blanch at requiring governments to purchase *Fanny Hill, Ulysses,* or the *Pentagon Papers.* By analogy, state officials may not ban a magazine with offensive language or refuse to allow a sexually explicit artwork to be shown, but this does not necessarily mean that they are required to fund the magazine or to provide a state-owned exhibit place for the artwork.[32] Even if this is debatable, qualitative judgments are an inherent part of the funding process—unless one's position is that the state must support all magazine publishers and struggling artists who seek state subsidies, if it supports any.[33]

IRREVOCABLE DELEGATIONS: DUE PROCESS AND THE FIRST AMENDMENT[34]

If the state has wide reign to select books and determine the curriculum, what mechanisms are there to limit the state's ability to indoctrinate without sacrificing its editorial powers? One answer is to strengthen private centers of communication, including the rights of students, teachers, and others to engage in speech on school premises so long as there is no undue disturbance of the state's own expression.[35] Both Professor Shiffrin and I have advocated this approach.[36] It is one thing to forbid a person wishing to speak on drug abuse to take over a gym class, and it is quite another to forbid him from distributing pamphlets on the problem in the school hallways between classes. But another way to think about the problem is to focus on what we mean by such fudge words as government, state, public officials, and the like. Governments are made up of people, and these people have different perspectives and different places in the hierarchy. The reality is that government communication powers and activities are so extensive that inevitably editorial responsibility is delegated to "professional" editors, those "street-level bureaucrats" responsible for the actual delivery of services. In the education context, the state legislature could vote on each book to be used in every school in the state, applying its editorial judgments. But in the nature of things authority is delegated to state departments of education, state textbook commissions, local school boards, principals, and even the teachers and school librarians themselves. This delegation of editorial authority, which often parallels the balkanization of governments responsible for education (the thousands of school districts and hundreds of thousands of schools, librarians, and teachers) is a bulwark against the centralized orchestration of a publicly established orthodoxy[37] that Justice Jackson warned us about nearly forty years ago.[38] Safety lies in keeping politicians too busy to intervene in daily decisions about book acquisitions or student newspaper articles, in the sense that professionals should make the judgments in custom and practice. What is to be feared is dilettante politicians and special-interest groups with political muscle.

The concept of delegated editorial responsibility is a powerful one. Consider, for example, the doctrine of academic freedom for teachers.[39] These cases seem difficult to justify,[40] and the Supreme Court has never embraced the right explicitly and distinguished it from traditional First Amendment doctrine.[41] Should the fortuity of speaking and teaching for a living entitle an instructor to some special autonomy that other government employees do not share?[42] Is it because they deal in words? And what of a librarian's asserted right to academic freedom? Why should a government employee who purchases books have any greater latitude than a government supply officer responsible for ordering paper and office equipment? Part of the answer, surely, is that books and words have a peculiarly important position in a democracy. But this could equally as well argue for greater supervision of teachers and librarians in public schools. What students learn is more important than which copying machine is purchased by a state highway department. And if the government is truly an editor, then why should not the government have the same rights of control and hiring and firing as private schools, newspapers, and broadcast stations?

The answer lies in the place which teachers and librarians occupy in the system of government expression, not per se in their own constitutional entitlements.[43] The greater the ability of higher echelon officials to control what goes on in each school, school library, and classroom, the greater the danger of the promulgation of a uniform message to its captive listeners. If teachers were automatons, required to adhere rigidly to lesson plans, book selections, and the like, ideological indoctrination could become a reality. If librarians were responsible only for processing book orders, with no discretion over what were ordered, the same risks could be incurred. In practice, varying discretion is given to teachers and librarians and the system works reasonably well. But what if editorial authority is not delegated to them? Is there a constitutional rule, derived from the First Amendment concern for government-established orthodoxy, that would require such delegations? In my own work, I have answered this question negatively.[44] If, for example, a school board establishes objective rules in advance that allow it to make judgments about textbook and library acquisitions, and if the school board in fact makes such decisions over time, then their decisionmaking apparatus is not subject to constitutional attack on the grounds that delegation and the division of authority over textbooks and library books is required.[45] But you should be aware of the fact that the student-newspaper cases implicitly reach a contrary result.[46] The conventional wisdom is that once a public school establishes a newspaper, although it need not have done so, it generally may not interfere with the editorial judgments of the student editors.[47] And the cases do not appear to turn on how much editorial discretion was given the students or whether faculty supervision was established in advance by objective rules.

How then does one explain cases like *Parducci* v. *Rutland*[48] in which Judge Johnson upheld the teacher's right to select a book for her students over the protestations of school authorities? *Cary* v. *Board of Education*,[49] a recent Tenth Circuit case, begins to unravel the answer. Judge Logan, in referring to *Parducci* and similar academic freedom cases, noted that

> the cases which held for the teachers and placed emphasis upon teachers' rights to exercise discretion in the classroom, seemed to be situations where school authorities acted in the absence of a general policy, after the fact, and had little to charge against the teacher other than the assignment with which they were unhappy.[50]

Thus, if higher authorities have no policy on book assignment or selection and thereby de facto delegate such authority to teachers and librarians, they cannot later intervene on an *ad hoc* basis to limit the dissemination of the books or their acquisition. Similarly, where school authorities have promulgated in advance a set of rules delegating authority to teachers, librarians, special textbook committees, and so forth, they should not be able to undo that delegation on a selective basis merely because they are dissatisfied with the results of that delegation in a particular instance.[51] In other words, the First Amendment should be construed to embody a doctrine of irrevocable delegations of authority in book selection policies, at least where the revocation operates retroactively or on an *ad hoc* basis.

The irrevocable delegation doctrine is rooted in Supreme Court opinions that require federal agencies to follow their own procedures, even if those procedures would not be constitutionally required in the first instance under the due process clause.[52] If one wishes to be technical about it, the argument might well be that established procedures for book selection and removal create a sort of property interest, settled and relied upon expectations as to how the state will behave, which are embodied in positive law. A student may not have a "right to know" and a publisher may have no right to government largesse, but they should have a right to compel a government entity to honor the procedures that have been established for determining what is taught and what books will be used. Less technically, an analogy may be drawn to the obscenity area where, as Professor Monaghan has noted, "the Court has placed little reliance upon the due process requirements of the Fifth and Fourteenth Amendments, but instead has turned directly to the First Amendment as the source of rules."[53] If the problem is that government communication in schools may overwhelm students, that in the process of learning they may lose their ability to think critically and independently, then the irrevocable delegation doctrine makes good sense. Courts are not put in the position of deciding what is propaganda or indoctrination and what is education. The state remains free to alter prospectively its decisional structure.[54] But having created a structure which is conducive to decentralized, balkanized, and professional decisionmaking about schoolbooks (whether intended or not), school authorities should be required to abide by that structure. If they wish to take on the job of editing the school curriculum and selecting books, it should be a full-time job. There should be no room for "Lone Rangers" who react to isolated book selection decisions, while ignoring the need to cultivate both community and individuality in the mass of curricular, library, and book assignment decisions.[55]

The irrevocability doctrine has not always been clearly applied by the courts. In the *Cary* case itself,[56] from which I just quoted, the school board had established a high school Language Arts Text Evaluation Committee to review materials for language arts courses. The committee consisted of teachers, administrators, parents, and students, and apparently it was charged with reporting its book recommendations to the school board. The books were not to be purchased by the district but by individual students. Only one book was rejected by a majority of the committee, but nine more were rejected in a minority. The school board approved 1275 books for the language arts classes, but rejected ten others—only six of which were listed in the minority report. The excluded books included *A Clockwork Orange* by Anthony Burgess, *The Exorcist* by William P. Blatty, *Coney Island of the Mind* by Lawrence Ferlinghetti, and *Kaddish and Other Poems* by Allen Ginsberg. The court upheld the expulsion, reasoning that if the board could decide not to offer contemporary poetry and if it could select the major textbook for the course, why could it not prevent the assignment of other books?[57] But with all due respect, that was not the question for review as the court had articulated it. The board established a review procedure, and it is not at all clear that the board abided by it. The case should have been remanded for such a determination. For example, was the board required to select books on the basis of the information provided by the majority and minority reports? If it was free to disregard all recommendations, then what was the point of the procedure? Was the board, like the committee members, required to follow objective standards and to give reasons for rejecting particular books? References to the general statutory powers of school boards do not answer these questions.[58]

Perhaps the most plausible explanation of the case is that the parties stipulated that the books were not obscene, that no systematic attempt had been made to exclude any particular philosophy, and that a "constitutionally proper decisionmaker" might well determine that the books were proper for high school language arts classes.[59] These stipulations may well have given away the game. The presumption of censorship of ideas that an *ad hoc* revocation of the committee's book selection authority normally entails, assuming that this was the case, was rebutted by plaintiffs' own concessions. The only plausible reason for nonselection was a judgment about the educational appropriateness of the books. Defendants conceded that students were not prohibited from reading the books and teachers were free to comment upon them and recommend them.[60] Only protracted discussion, which would in effect reinstate the forbidden books, was prohibited. But even so, the *Cary* court should have held the board to its own rules, thereby retaining a structure preservative of Fifth Amendment values and satisfying the expectations of the participants.

In contrast to *Cary*, the court in *Salvail v. Nashua Board of Education*[61] relied heavily on the failure of the board of education to follow its own procedures[62] in a decision to remove all and then parts of *Ms.* magazine from the school library. In that case the board approved guidelines for the selection of instructional materials, delegating its editorial function to the "professionally trained personnel employed by the school district."[63] The guidelines contained criteria for selection, including quality of presentation, appropriateness for age, subject, and ability levels, and literary quality. The guidelines also provided that the chosen books should help students be aware of the contributions of both sexes and of various religious, ethnic, and subcultural groups, and that on controversial issues, the collection should be balanced and insure the representation of various religious, ethnic, and cultural groups; and that on controversial issues, the collection should be balanced and insure the representation of various points of view. In the event of a citizen complaint or question about book selection, the guidelines provided for appeals to an Instructional Materials Reconsideration Committee, with subsequent appeals to the superintendent and school board.[64] Bypassing these procedures a board member presented a formal resolution to remove *Ms.* magazine from the school library, and this was approved by the board despite the protestations of the superintendent that the established procedures should be followed. The court held that the board "was required to follow [the guidelines] in its attempt at removal of *Ms.* magazine from the shelves of the high school library."[65] This conclusion of law was sufficient to support the court injunction against banning the magazine from the school library. It was unnecessary for the court to address broader censorship issues, relating to whether the alleged "sexual overtones" of the magazine were simply a pretext for banning an objectional point of view.[66]

This last point is worthy of elaboration. The remedy for violating preestablished book selection and removal policies should be the acquisition or reshelving of the books in question. There are other possibilities. The board might decide or be ordered to submit the book for review through the existing procedures. But this is time consuming and the passage of time alone might well sustain the board's original unlawful action. Further, the knowledge of the board's previous decision might well taint the decisionmaking processes of the selection committee. Many members of the selection committee are likely to be school employees. And even the promulgation of new policies empowering the board to make such decisions, and applying these policies prospectively, invites disingenuous behavior with respect to the specific books that have been at the center of controversy. In other words, an effective deterrent needs to be created, and a requirement of further proceedings would not create such a deterrent.

BOOK SELECTION AND PROCEDURAL DUE PROCESS

Apart from bolstering the delegation of authority, one may think about applying more traditional due process techniques to the book selection process. I have found only one case adopting this position, *Loewen v. Turnipseed*,[67] a district court case arising in the Northern District of Mississippi. In that case the "rating committee" appointed by the governor and state superintendent of education of Mississippi approved a book entitled *Your Mississippi* for purchase by the State Textbook Purchasing Board and disapproved a book entitled *Mississippi: Conflict and Change*. The books were considered for use in ninth-grade classes in Mississippi history, and apparently the state would purchase approved books for both public and parochial schools. The controversy arose because *Mississippi: Conflict and Change* allegedly emphasized the mistreatment of blacks in Mississippi, while the alternative selection did not. The "rating committee" split on the issue, with the white majority outvoting the black minority. The court ultimately held that the selection was motivated by racial discrimination, intended to perpetuate segregation, and was therefore unconstitutional.[68]

But along the way the court held that the rating committee procedure for selecting textbooks was also unconstitutional. Mississippi law did not provide for review of the rating committee's decision, "without giving those adversely affected by it a voice in the matter."[69] Since the publishers of the books were given an opportunity to present their positions to the committee, presumably the court had in mind the authors, and students, faculty, and school districts across the state. And indeed they were the plaintiffs. At first blush the holding appears difficult to sustain. In the jargon, the decision appears to be a legislative and not an adjudicative matter.[70] A governmental body is not constitutionally required to hold an adversary hearing in deciding to award a construction contract for a public building. But perhaps, as in the case of the irrevocable delegation doctrine, guidance should be sought more in First Amendment interests than in the due process clause.[71] A loose parallel may be found in the obscenity cases where adversary hearings are required, notwithstanding the fact that the publisher's property interest alone would not justify such stringent procedural safeguards.[72]

The stigma[73] or now-stigma[74] plus cases decided under the due process clause may also provide a rough parallel. Where governmental communications may stigmatize a person and where he is simultaneously deprived of some entitlement, the government may be required to hold a hearing to determine the facts of the matter. The notion is that a liberty interest has been violated. A classic case would be the dismissal of a public employee, accompanied by publicized charges that he had engaged in some reprehensible behavior.[75]

I have argued elsewhere that these cases are best understood from the perspective of government expression that may do untold damage to an individual's life chances.[76] In a modern industrial society, widely publicized government accusations may do as much harm to a person as the loss of liberty through incarceration or the taking of his physical property. A hearing requirement does not mean that the government may not speak badly about individuals, but only that, under some circumstances, it must abide by procedures designed to insure the accuracy of the government's remarks. In Loewen, government is expressing itself through its textbook selections. The potential harm to authors, students, and others is great, and perhaps a due process hearing makes sense despite the lack of fit between these facts and prior due process decisions.

While I am dubious about this aspect of Loewen surviving appellate review, it is clear that even affirmance would require the adoption of some limiting principle. Surely, governments are not required to hold a due process hearing every time they wish to make a decision about funding research, purchasing a book, subsidizing the arts, or publishing a manuscript at the Government Printing Office. One tentative suggestion is that a distinction might be drawn between books that may be marketed only in schools and those that have a more general market. That is, in the case of textbooks an adverse decision is financially devastating and the book is unlikely to be read widely. For novels by Graham Greene or Howard Fast, the impact is far less grave. Thus, a hearing might be required for textbook selections, whereas it would not be required for the general run of books acquired by school libraries.

Finally, I cannot resist making one last point about the Loewen case. The court did not order the rating committee to alter its procedures to conform to its opinion. Rather, as in Cary, the court enjoined the defendants to approve Mississippi: Conflict and Change.[77] The practical result of the case was that both books under consideration were approved and local Mississippi school districts and dioceses were free to choose the one they preferred. This is indeed a Solomonic remedy. But more importantly, the decision effectively placed the power to make textbook selections in the hands of local communities and local school officials. Not only is this consistent with the irrevocable delegation doctrine, but it also has overtones of structural due process.[78] Perhaps, as in the Supreme Court's pornography,[79] school financing,[80] and zoning cases,[81] the district court intended to emphasize the need for community and not statewide decisionmaking.[82] If schools are to reflect the values of the communities in which they are located, then each community should be able to determine its own standards for schoolbooks. Parents and publishers do not decide, but neither should distant state officials. While I admit that the constitutional underpinnings of the argument are subject to question, community decisionmaking is consistent both with the mission of schools and with the First Amendment interest in avoiding wholesale indoctrination through a centralized decisionmaking process.

ILLICIT MOTIVATION

In a number of fascinating recent decisions, circuit courts have gone a full step further than the irrevocable delegation doctrine. They have sought to distinguish good faith pedagogic judgments about books from an effort to indoctrinate to a particular school of thought or political point of view.[83] This is a task of immense difficulty, largely dependent on a motivational analysis. In my own writing, I have been skeptical about such efforts except in situations where the state cannot even plausibly argue that it is pursuing the goal of education.[84] Professor Shiffrin, on the other hand, sees more possibilities in this approach,[85] and the weight of authority appears, at the moment, to be more consistent with this approach.[86] Perhaps the best exposition of the principle occurred in the *Zykan* case:

> [T]he Constitution [does not] permit the courts to interfere with local educational discretion until local authorities begin to substitute rigid and exclusive indoctrination for the mere exercise of their prerogative to make pedagogic choices regarding matters of legitimate dispute.
>
> Noticeably absent from the amended complaint is any hint that the decisions of these administrators flow from . . . some systematic effort to exclude a particular type of thought, or even from some identifiable ideological preference.[87]

Not surprisingly, the court remanded the case to allow amendment of the pleadings and presentation of evidence on the motivation issue.[88]

The *Warsaw* case is rather complex. Essentially, the student plaintiffs filed suit under Section 1983 alleging that their First and Fourteenth Amendment rights had been violated by a series of related school board decisions. A textbook was removed from the school premises (values clarification) and given to a senior citizens' group for public burning. Four books ordered for a Women in Literature course (*Growing Up Female in America, Go Ask Alice, The Bell Jar,* and *The Stepford Wives*) were not permitted to be used. The school board, under a new policy prohibiting reading materials that might be objectionable, also excised portions of *Student Critic* and permanently removed *Go Ask Alice* from the school library. Adding icing to the cake, the established school procedures for book selection decisions were not followed, seven courses were eliminated from the curriculum, and the English teacher who planned to offer the Women in Literature course was not rehired.[89] The plaintiffs alleged that these actions were largely taken because particular words in the books offended the school board's social, political, and moral tastes.[90] The court found this insufficient, however, because school boards are supposed to act on such tastes and beliefs in making book selection, curricular, and other decisions. In the court's words,

> The amended complaint nowhere suggests that in taking these actions defendants have been guided by an interest in imposing some religious or scientific orthodoxy to eliminate a particular kind of inquiry generally.[91]

Apparently, if one is to credit the court's account of the case, plaintiffs erred in not specifically alleging that the board was attempting to eliminate feminist thought from the public schools.[92]

With all my reservations about the workability of the motivation test, the court's treatment of the facts and pleadings in *Zykan* is bizarre. The court might have held that all public education casts a pall of orthodoxy and eliminates some kinds of inquiries. That is its purpose. If anthropology books and courses are not available in the schools, a sort of orthodoxy and limit on inquiry is evident. But the court had a case in which a series of books relating to feminism were banished, the school board short-circuited normal procedures for book selection and retention, and the teacher who proposed to discuss the banned books lost her job. If there is a distinction between imposed orthodoxy and education, the Warsaw community board clearly was on the wrong side of the distinction.

From any reasonable perspective, *Zykan* illustrates the type of facts that shed light on a school board's motivation to censor or edit. First, there was a series of related, but nonetheless *ad hoc* determinations, all of which pointed in the direction of eliminating feminist thought from the schools.[93] Second, the book decisions clearly did not rest on considerations of economy or scarce resources. Third, the school board was not selecting among disciplines or subjects so much as it was addressing itself to a current political issue that cut across many disciplines. Fourth, the reasonable evidentiary presumption that the failure of the board to abide by its own procedures is a sign that it is engaging in censorship was not rebutted by the extrinsic evidence.[94] Fifth, the removal of a book from a library and the nonrenewal of a teacher lends itself better to motivational analysis. In a sense, it is easier to figure out why someone was fired or why a book was removed than it is to determine why someone was hired among hundreds of applicants or why a book was not purchased from the thousands available.[95] This is consistent with the *Minarcini* decision,[96] distinguishing book acquisition and book removal policies.

In this multifactored motivational analysis, *Zykan* indicates that courts should not decide school book controversies without detailed examination of the facts. As a general matter, judges should not be dismissing complaints with prejudice or rendering summary decisions if they are to take seriously their extremely difficult task. And certainly plaintiffs should not move for summary judgment and should resist all of defendants' efforts to short-cut the fact-finding process. Beyond this, however, *Zykan* reveals precious little about what the lower court should do with those facts. With some hesitancy, let me propose a legal text. Borrowing from the racial discrimination context,[97] the standard should be whether the defendants would have taken the action they in fact took, but for the illegitimate desire to suppress objectionable and controversial ideas.[98] While perhaps orthodoxy and education cannot be easily distinguished, the point may well be that the effort to censor, rather than to edit, is a corruption of the political processes by which schooling decisions are made.[99] In any given case, the impact of censorship and editing may be the same (for example, Russian history books are not read in schools), but the polity has a strong interest in insuring that the intergenerational communication of knowledge and values is not guided by principles inconsistent with democratic and First Amendments precepts relating to the creation of self-controlled citizens.

In my view, the leading case on removal of books from public school libraries, *Pico v. Board of Education, Island Trees Union Free School District*,[100] is consistent with the standard that I have articulated. *Pico* involves such outlandish and bizarre official behavior that it would be difficult (but not impossible) for any court to resist some form of intervention. The case involved the removal of ten books from school libraries, including *The Fixer, Slaughterhouse-Five, The Naked Ape, Soul on Ice,* and others. As Judge Sifton noted with amusing understatement, this was accomplished through "unusual and irregular intervention in school libraries' operations by persons not routinely concerned with their contents." Three school board members had attended a conference sponsored by a conservative organization and had obtained a copy of a list of objectionable books. The list was annotated with remarks that particular books were seditious, disloyal, anti-white women, anti-Christian, and pro-feminist. Sensing an emergency, two of the board members gained entry to a school library at night and found ten of the most objectionable books in the card catalog. Over the objections of the superintendent, the board then bypassed normal selection and removal procedures and banned the books. The removal became a *cause célèbre*, and the incumbent board members were reelected, in part at least because of their stance on the book removal issue. After the suit was filed, defendants emphasized that their decision was premised on "the repellent and vulgar language present in the books." Not surprisingly, Judge Sifton did not believe them. Judge Newman was not sure, and he and Judge Sifton ordered the case remanded for full trial (the case arose as an appeal from the granting of summary judgment for defendants). Judge Mansfield dissented.

Judge Sifton's opinion could not be more to the point. He did not for a moment deny the socialization function of public schools. And socialization inevitably involves the suppression of some facts and ideas. But his view was that the facts gave rise to "an inference . . . that political views and personal taste are being asserted not in the interests of the children's well-being, but rather for the purpose of establishing those views as the correct and orthodox ones for all purposes in the particular community." Thus, it was clear that the defendants would not have removed the books but for the desire to impose an orthodoxy and to suppress inconsistent ideas. The decisionmaking process of the school system had been corrupted by an effort "to express an official policy with regard to God and country. . . ." If the school board had been interested in an editing process designed to ferret out educationally inappropriate reading matter, many of the same books might well have been removed. But the similarity of impact of censorship and editing would not obviate a motive so patently inconsistent with First Amendment values. Judge Newman said much the same thing, opining that education may sometimes involve the suppression of ideas. But he could not accept such suppression "when exclusion of particular views is motivated by the authorities' opinion about the proper way to organize and run society in general." But given the defendants' formally expressed reasons for removing the books, he courteously insisted that a full trial was necessary "to determine precisely what happened."

Bicknell v. *Vergennes Union High School Board*[101] was decided by the same panel on the same day as *Pico*, and it also involved the removal of books from the school library. This time, however, Judge Newman changed his vote and affirmed the lower court's dismissal of the complaint for failure to state a claim upon which relief could be granted. Judge Mansfield concurred, and Judge Sifton dissented. My impression is that Judge Newman wished to illuminate the law by contrasting the results in *Pico* and *Bicknell*, and to create one of those "but see" or "compare" footnotes that would gain immortality in the pages of law reviews and law reports. In any event, the defendant board had created a "School Library Bill of Rights for School Library Media Center Program"; and this document gave the professional staff the "right" "to freely select, in accordance with Board policy, organize and administer the media collection to best serve teachers and students." If a complaint were received about a staff book selection, the librarian was to attempt to resolve the matter. Any unresolved matters were for the board. Without following the procedure, the board, upon complaint, removed *Dog Day Afternoon* and *The Wanderers* from the school library, asserting that they employed "vulgar and indecent language." The board also voted to prohibit the librarian from purchasing any additional major works of fiction, and required that library purchases in other areas be reviewed by both the school administration and the board. Subsequent to these actions, a number of students, parents, and library employees and the Right to Read Defense Fund brought suit.

To begin with the obvious, the facts of *Bicknell* are much less compelling from the plaintiffs' standpoint than those in *Pico*. The board's actions appear to be much less of an ideological witch-hunt, and there is nothing about the decision to review books jointly in the future that violates First Amendment doctrine.[102] But the most straightforward explanation of *Bicknell* is that it is a pleading case. While plaintiffs claimed that the board's action was motivated "by personal tastes and values,"[103] they did not assert (according to Judge Newman) that the removal of the books was motivated by political concerns. They admitted "that the books were removed because of vulgarity and obscenity." The plaintiffs also claimed that the failure of the school board to follow its own procedures was a violation of due process of law. Judge Newman, while not commenting on the district court's finding to the contrary, held as a matter of law that the claim was without merit. Judge Sifton agreed in his dissenting opinion, but argued that these procedural irregularities should be explored at trial in the context of determining the motivation of the board.

In my view, *Bicknell* is wrongly decided under applicable constitutional doctrines. As in *Cary*,[104] if the plaintiffs did not use the magic words about motivation to achieve political orthodoxy, they should have had an opportunity to amend their complaint or refile the suit with the appropriate pleadings. Again, if the Second Circuit is going into the motivation business with regard to book selection and removal policies (I tried to warn them),[105] summary procedures are entirely inappropriate. If the motives were mixed, and according to Judge Newman the plaintiffs unwisely conceded on the obscenity issue, there still is the question of whether the removal would have occurred but for a political motivation to suppress ideas. Further, both Judges Sifton and Newman did not clearly articulate or understand the irrevocable delegation doctrine. Judge Newman opines that the sort of right recognized in *Pico*, presumably a right to avoid ideologically motivated official efforts to suppress ideas through book selections, is not the sort of interest in liberty or property that typically gives rise to a requirement for a due process hearing.[106] Judge Sifton agreed. Even if *Loewen* were the law of the land, which it is not,[107] I agree. But the entitlement is not a property or liberty interest in avoiding orthodoxy; it is the property and liberty interest, combined with First Amendment values, in assuring that a school board follows its own procedures for removing library books. The emphasis on procedural due process in its usual sense and not in the sense of reinforcing the board's delegation of selection and removal functions is a fundamental error in the decision. And this causes the judges to ignore the value of decentralized, balkanized, and professional decisionmaking in advancing First Amendment values.

RESERVATIONS AND REFLECTIONS

Having examined the recent case law on book selection and removal policies, permit me to make a number of observations and to express a certain uneasiness. The irrevocable delegation doctrine strikes me as the wisest compromise in terms of avoiding the quagmire of motivation theory and in terms of playing to the demonstrated competencies of courts. On the other hand, it is not as protecting of First Amendment values as other approaches, and it invites school boards to take on limited review functions that may meet the letter, if not the spirit, of the doctrine. And the constitutional status of the doctrine is not assured, with some recent Supreme Court *dicta* pointing in the opposite direction.[108] With regard to traditional due process guarantees, recent Supreme Court decisions do not bode well for their extension even to a limited class of book selection cases.[109] The Court also has shown an inclination to dilute the remedies for the failure to follow due process procedures,[110] and reinstatement of rejected books may be much too much for it to swallow. Interestingly enough, the structural due process approach, requiring that local communities make book decisions, is highly consistent with the prevailing philosophy of many of the Justices. But the precedents are few, they are easily distinguishable, and it is far from certain the Court will be impressed by the structural due process writings of such distinguished scholars as Laurence Tribe and Professor (now Judge) Hans Linde.[111]

But for all of these doubts, I believe it remains an open question as to whether the sorts of lines which the Second and Seventh Circuits have sought to draw are workable or desirable. How does one know an "orthodoxy" when one sees one? Is not all education centered on establishing certain orthodoxies and editing out of the curriculum ideas and facts which are deemed wrong or unimportant by the community? To raise a specific example, the *Pico, Bicknell, Zykan,* and *Salvail* decisions all assume that the exclusion of sexually oriented books or books with dirty words is constitutionally permissible. But why is this not as much of an imposition of values as is implicit in the exclusion of a feminist or a civil rights point of view? Is not the inculcation of standards of morality and sexual behavior one of the purposes of public schooling? Or is it, as the court in *Right to Read Defense Committee v. School Committee of the City of Chelsea*,[112] that school boards should have no constitutional power to remove an allegedly offensive library book unless the book meets constitutional standards of obscenity?[113] But is this not inconsistent with the accepted notion that school authorities may pass on the educational appropriateness of books for youngsters in the schools, with the notion that the vast majority of people in a particular community may not wish their sons and daughters subjected to such materials?

There is also the danger that courts will intrude too far into the curriculum of public schools, and that there will be a loss of accountability for book selection and removal decisions. At the moment this danger appears remote. Whatever the articulated standard, plaintiffs have gained few victories. And a few well publicized victories may well do more to influence school officials than a multitude of losses. But this suggests to me what everyone should realize. The primary restraints on excessive government communication activities are political and attitudinal.[114] Restraint depends on the independence of private publishers and their willingness to do political battle over their First Amendment beliefs. It depends on persuading public officials and the public itself that censorship is not the way. It depends on revitalizing our traditions of local control of education and on keeping state and federal governments as far removed as possible from school book decisions. In the last analysis, people will have the kind of schools that they want and deserve.

Current Law, Future Legal Theories, a Panel Discussion

Panelists: Mark G. Yudof, Vincent Blasi, and William Van Alstyne

THE ISSUE OF DELEGATION

Mr. Yudof:

Someone said that the paradigm of a government worker today is probably the school teacher and not the postal employee, who actually does something physical. That is, the government is massively in the business of communicating in all sorts of sectors.

Let me try to discuss some of the major points of the paper, and then try to indicate some areas where I make massive retreat. What I was essentially trying to do was work through as many different theories as you could utilize in litigating these cases. Admittedly, along the way I added some editorial comments, such as "This isn't going to fly," or "I really don't believe this." It is an area which requires particularized inquiry into doctrine. What are the sorts of theories that I would try to exhaust if I were representing a client who was, for example, upset about a book being removed from a library, a teacher being fired for recommending a particular reading, or a similar situation?

My view is that disentangling something called indoctrination from something called education, or simply communicating ideas or knowledge and processes of persuasion, is an extremely difficult task. I have spent a great deal of time reading the communications literature and books about what is called the propaganda literature, which began shortly after World War I, by Laswell and others. One of the things you see in the literature is that there is no such thing as value-free education. Even if you are teaching an arithmetic class, the very examples that you use may promote capitalism, as may the mere fact that you are teaching American history rather than Russian history, the American Constitution rather than the Communist Manifesto.

A second problem is that frequently in this propaganda literature the real difference relates to the sorts of values that are being communicated. And that is evidenced by the expression that one man's truth is another's propaganda. That is, when people began pushing hard enough on this propaganda versus education distinction, frequently they came to the conclusion that they just didn't like what was being taught in Nazi Germany schools or in Soviet schools and that when values of tolerance and free expression, free exercise of religion, and the like were being taught, those were the sorts of values with which they could live.

Another aspect of this is that if you think in terms of the philosophic distinction between affirmative and negative freedom, education acts in a sense to both contract and expand the mind. If people are not aware of their existing institutions, if they don't have facility with the language, if they don't know how Newtonian physics works, if they are not familiar with history, presumably it is very difficult for them to progress beyond those things, to theories of relativity, to new breakthroughs in terms of the arts, the humanities, science or whatever. The very process of communication by which we learn that particular words have particular meanings is one which is limiting. Presumably we are in part captive to our culture, and that culture is reflected in the schools.

There are plenty of studies which show that a lot which is learned in school is not even in the official curriculum. And that has to do with rules of decorum, rules of dress, rules of waiting one's turn, and the like. Also, no matter how it is cast, all the studies show a profound respect for founding fathers—not mothers—appreciation of the nation, its institutions, its electoral processes, and the like. Even given variations in presentations, that is a lot of what children learn when they are exposed to these sorts of materials.

This process which I have described is one of education, but also one of indoctrination; and it is in a practical, political, and legal sense legitimate. The decision to have public schools that are publicly operated, with legislatures passing laws as to what will be taught, the decision to certify teachers, the whole panoply of compulsoriness and requirements, is inherently antiliberal. It is antiliberal in the sense that there is vast potential for indoctrination. One of the things one can do with that, I suppose, is to take a John Stewart Mill approach and engage in a sort of frontal attack. That is, the problem is that the schools indoctrinate. The problem isn't per se the choice among textbooks, the choice among teachers, and the like in

any given instance. It is that the whole enterprise is rotten.
It rests upon antiliberal assumptions about the need to socialize people to particular norms.

Another way to approach it is to try to probe to the limits
of that indoctrination process. That is, not to explore what I
think is a naive distinction between inculcating values and
teaching or transmitting information, but to see if we can
think about either structural or other limitations which may
deal with some of the more blatant, outrageous examples of
misuse of this power. I don't think that at a pragmatic level
one can say that it is for publishers, or for children, to decide
what is taught in the public schools. Teaching and curriculum, like a newspaper or like public television, inherently
involves an editing process that inevitably has an impact on
the socialization process. Furthermore, you have the compli-
cated captive-audience problem. That is, there can be an
incompatibility between the assertion of private rights and
the public mission as it has been identified. The most obvious
example is someone who decides to conduct a full-blown discussion of American foreign policy in a geometry class. Obviously, that may be a First Amendment sort of entitlement, but
it is inconsistent with carrying out the mission of the geometry class. So too, the state, if it is to carry out its mission—
unless you are to attack its legitimacy and ask if it is legitimate
for it to have schools, if it is legitimate for it to transmit
knowledge and values—it has to perform this editing process.
So, if schools are public forums, or open forums, or whatever
you call them, then they cannot accomplish that objective.

One of the things that struck me is that, in fact, decisions
in schools and elsewhere in government are frequently delegated to what have been called "street-level bureaucrats"—
that is, the people who actually deliver the services. They
may be editors of the *Rutgers Law Journal*, they may be teachers, they may be psychiatrists, they may be librarians. One of
the fortunate facts of life is that politicians only have so much
time. That is, it is possible for a legislative committee to
review every book that is going to be assigned in the whole
state of New York, but it is not a task for which the committee
has any great taste. It is that lack of taste, interest, and inclination which is an enormous safety factor. So, one of the things
I thought about is how nice it would be if we could strengthen
those historic delegations of authority to the teachers, the
librarians, the local managers, the local public television station, and the like. By doing that, one balkanizes the decisionmaking process and makes it less possible to achieve a sort of

uniformity of view. It is a good idea not to have a ministry of propaganda or education. It is probably better to have 11,000 school districts.

The doctrine I suggested was that if the authority had been delegated, either on a *de facto* or *de jure* basis, then the *ad hoc* and selective repudiation of the delegation could provide a basis for some judicial relief. That is, as Frankfurter said in one of his famous decisions, "He who grasps for the procedural sword may very well die by the procedural sword." I thought that it was a good idea in this case to hold the authorities to that delegation of authority, to say that they have established voluntarily a structure which is protective of First Amendment interests and not allow them to act retroactively—not allow them to say they never review textbooks but are going to do this one, they never review optional assignments by the teachers but are going to review this particular one—and use that as a way to give protection to these First Amendment interests.

I do admit that it is possible that school boards and others will learn to play by the rules of the game. One problem with that, of course, is that they have to be willing to bear that burden. It is quite an onerous burden and I suspect that what one would see is more in the way of cycles. That is, you would see a case which perhaps is lost for failure to follow the procedures, followed by a change in the procedures. Then for a short time the review power would be taken seriously, followed by a *de facto* delegation of authority as the board members say they are just not paid enough, there are not enough hours in the week to sit and look at all these wretched books.

Another technique that I thought long and hard about came out of the *Loewen*[1] case, which I think is an absolutely fascinating case. I began to think about the question of procedural due process. In the *Loewen* case the court seemed to say that at the state level and at the rating commission perhaps various interests had to be represented. It appeared to me that in *Loewen* the court was requiring an adversary hearing when they were in the process of reviewing textbooks and when, in particular, they were going to deny funding for a particular textbook. That is, they would not select one for which the state would pay and from which the local communities could choose.

I think that is a difficult sort of argument; it doesn't fit squarely with the "new liberty" and the "new property." That is because there is the "new, new property," and the "new, new liberty." Obviously, as Bill Van Alstyne has written, there has been some movement in the Supreme Court, which would not seem to indicate any tremendous outpouring of sympathy for new procedural protections of this sort. It would guarantee some sort of access to the decisionmaking structure, but it doesn't fit well with the traditional due process cases, and I think probably you need some sort of limiting principle. It can't be the case that anytime the state, for example, refuses to buy a book, someone can call and say, "I am here from the 'X' Publishing Company. I noticed that you ordered one hundred books last month. We are among the 9,900 that you did not order, and we want a due process hearing on that issue." The question is, As a practical matter, under what circumstances would you allow for the triggering of such a hearing? It strikes me that if we are going to take this procedural route, we need some limiting principle. The other problem with this, of course, is that we normally require hearings by the state of other construction contracts and the like as a matter of constitutional law. The question of where this fits in Judge Friendly's typography of administrative versus legislative versus judicial adjudicative hearings and the like is not entirely clear.[2]

A third technique which I found appealing, but which has markedly little support other than in Professor Tribe's *American Constitutional Law* book, is a theory of structural due process and, believe it or not, I also found that in the *Loewen* case. If you look at the remedy in *Loewen*, what they essentially held was that the disapproval of this book was unconstitutional and that therefore it had to be included on the list of books for which the state would pay at least for the ninth-grade history course. As a result, there was a sort of local option; that is, each community got to choose among these books and, in fact, some of the plaintiffs were involved in both public and parochial school systems that apparently were willing to opt for the disapproved books. The idea here would be, I suppose, that if schools are to reflect community values, if the danger is one of an overarching indoctrination and censorship, then perhaps it is communities that should make that decision. It is neither the parent nor the child, on one hand, nor the state authorities on the other, who should make the decision. The power should be placed somewhere in between at the community level. The Supreme Court, in a quite different context, I admit, has tended to place the power there in the pornography cases. It is the community's standards, not the statewide standards. In the school financing case (which I lost, so I'm very aware of that), they tended to put the power again in the local communities. In some of the zoning cases, like *Village of Belle Terre*,[3] they talked about a community defining its own ambiance and population and the like. And there are cases like *Yoder*[4] and others. I'm not sure how strong the constitutional arguments are, and there are a couple of cases which Tribe cites, but the point would be to try to use a structural due process argument to place the power in local communities and, I suppose, to declare unconstitutional the schemes in twenty some states that place that power in state textbook commissions.

The last argument that I considered, and the one which I think we've talked most about, had to do with a sort of illicit motivation theory. That is, as I read the cases, the courts—at least the *Warsaw*[5] court, the *Pico*[6] court, and in the language of *Bicknell*[7]—have sought to distinguish between good faith pedagogic judgments about books, perhaps about courses, from an effort to indoctrinate to a particular school of thought or political point of view. And on that sort of motivation test—whether the court viewing the facts would describe this as a good faith educational judgment for the benefit of the children or as a program to indoctrinate to a particular ideology—the result in the case would hinge. It seemed that the courts were saying that it depended where your personal tastes were directed. If you were exercising your best judgment in a pedagogical mode, and it involved your taste, that was all right. But if you were expressing your taste, best judgment, and so forth in your political mode, your ideological or indoctrinational mode, then that was not all right. I have been reluctant to get into this sort of motivational analysis for some of the reasons I've already stated. I think that the lines are difficult to draw. I think that I agree partially with Professor Van Alstyne that there are some analogies to the establishment clause. But the establishment clause is really the only direct substantive limit in the Constitution on government expression. In other words, we don't have a clause which says you may not establish, for example, a political ideology. We have a clause which has been interpreted to mean you may not establish a religious ideology. So that's clearly one difference. Obviously, there may be some analogy in distinguishing between the school prayer cases and let's teach about religion, and clearly the court said that in the *Schempp*[8] case. I once had Mrs. O'Hair in my class and she said that she would love to teach about religion in the public schools and that she, too, read the case the same way. The courts have had a very difficult time with some of this—with moments of silence, meditation, and so on. The other thing is that we had what amounted to a ritual very similar to *West Virginia State Board of Education* v. *Barnette.*[9] We had a ritual which seemed to have no virtue other than to indoctrinate. Unlike the ritual of reciting a mathematics table of some sort, or the ritual of memorizing a poem, this is a somewhat different sort of thing, and it's not quite as easy to draw the line.

In *Zykan*, there was a series of related, but nonetheless *ad hoc*, determinations, all of which pointed in the direction of eliminating feminist thought from the schools. Second, there was really no plausible argument that was made on grounds of economy or scarce resources or anything of that order. Third, and this is where it gets very tricky, the school board didn't seem to be selecting among disciplines or subjects. This was not a decision to teach economics rather than anthropology; it seemed to be directly addressing itself to current political issues which cut across all these other areas in the school curriculum. So, perhaps the relationship to the electoral process of pending policy determinations and the like had something to do with it.

Fourth, there was nothing in the case which rebutted what I considered to be the strong presumption that if you violate your own procedures and you step in on some content-related basis, that smacks more of something people would call censorship. And fifth, of course, this was the removal not only of a book from a library, the so-called tenured book problem; but this was also the removal of a teacher, in this case the nontenured teacher problem. Without going into detail, I think I agree with the proposition that it's often easier as an evidentiary matter to try to figure out why something that was already there, be it a teacher or a book, was taken out than it is to figure out why one decision among 100,000 was made at the outset.

Shortcutting the fact-finding process from the plaintiff's perspective is probably a very, very bad idea. If these cases are going to turn on this motivational analysis, a concession that they weren't out to indoctrinate, that they didn't have a particular political perspective, is likely to lead to an adverse determination of the litigation. I suppose the standard which I would borrow from the race cases is to ask whether the defendants, in the light of all the facts, would have taken this action but for the illegitimate desire to suppress objectionable and controversial ideas. It is a sort of "but for" analysis, a very difficult test. But if we're really persuaded that the process was corrupted by these illegitimate concerns—

illegitimate because they're inconsistent with the notion of a self-controlled citizen who participates in this marketplace of ideas and who makes up his or her own mind about policy matters—then perhaps we should intervene even though under other circumstances, if this decision were editorial and pedagogic in nature, the same result might be permissible.

One last point . . . demonstrates some of the difficulties with this notion of an "orthodoxy" in the exclusion of sexually orientated books with four-letter words and the like, which gives rise to many of these cases—perhaps eighty percent of the complaints at the local level. This involves us in the matter of limiting indoctrination in the schools. Because you can plausibly make the argument that if it is indoctrination to exclude a feminist, civil rights, or black point of view in the schools, that it is indoctrination to take out the dirty words or remove the books containing the dirty words, then there is a message conveyed by forbidding books which describe sexual activity or contain particular types of words. It seems to me that the *Pico*, the *Bicknell*, the *Zykan*, and the *Salvail*[10] courts all seemed to miss this point. They seem to be saying, "Well, if you're checking to impose an ideology, you can't do that; but if you just want to get the dirty words out, that's fine, because all you're doing there is deciding what's appropriate for children." But, as in the *Chelsea* case,[11] the argument could be made that the decision about whether or not something is appropriate in terms of its use of four-letter words or its descriptions of appropriate or inappropriate sexual conduct, itself conveys an ideology. And how does one distinguish that ideology from the sort of ideology that the court said in *Pico*, for example, would be objectionable? There are a large number of people—and hence the conflict—who think that the schools should be conveying these moral values. In their view the family is not good enough. Essentially their position is that the state should be inculcating the values of the majority.

THE LIMITS OF INDOCTRINATION

Mr. Blasi:

I want to divide Mark's paper into two levels. One is what Bill Van Alstyne, in a fetching phrase, called the "infinitely difficult but merely practical questions." And the other is what I would call the theoretical underpinnings. What Mark says about those is a good deal more subtle. I'm going to try to tease out a little of that at the risk of taking liberties with his thought.

For almost any area of robust constitutional doctrine, the norms can roughly be divided into two kinds. One is what you might call "substantive norms," where you read the Constitution as embodying actual values that have a certain bite, that are not simply consensus values but have a certain thrust. The other for more common underpinning of a robust constitutional doctrine is what you might call the "process norms." This describes the bulk of our constitutional doctrine. A certain area is defined as sensitive or important not because you perceive a particular specified value to be encroached upon, but because the topic seems to be the sort of thing that the Constitution deals with. Once you've defined the area by topic as special, then the norms you invoke are more consensual. They are norms like self-consistency, coherency, fairness in a very capacious sense, and efficacy. That is, it's a bit like what happens in the equal protection area under what's called strict scrutiny. Since this area is pretty important—these kinds of distinctions are sensitive based on alienage, race, or whatever—we are going to be absolutely certain that the legislature is consistent and efficacious. We're not going to impose any ideology or substantive norms, but we're going to look very closely at the process aspect of it. What happens, at the strategy level is that we're trying to hoist the legislature or the governmental decisionmaker by its own petard. We say they've committed themselves to this; if they're serious about it, then they should have acted this way. They didn't and therefore either they weren't serious about it or fumbled it.

Let's focus on the process norms. Professor Yudof suggests some substantive norms, but I think he backs off every time he tries to elaborate on what those substantive norms might be and how they might produce workable legal theories. He suggests what strikes me as an interesting shift of focus away from indoctrination versus education and toward a distinction between censorship and editing. But I think his final remarks reflect doubt that this distinction will ever really blossom as a fruitful source of legal theory. Professor Yudof leaves us with the idea that the most promising avenue is the "irrevocable delegation" doctrine and that we should look toward these kinds of process norms.

I have some problems with that. Take the irrevocable delegation doctrine, which is the most promising process norm that he develops. There are real problems with that. If you make the concession that schools are in large part about indoctrination, then it is not really hoisting the school board or the state board of education by its own petard when you prove that in essence they have come up with *ad hoc* policies to exclude certain kinds of books. I think what Mark is saying is that there's a neutral-principles norm that has to be applied to decisionmaking relating to the inculcation of values inherent in the socialization process. That is, you've got to come up with your procedures in advance; you've got to operate at a certain level of generality. It's the *ad hoc, ex post facto* decision relating to socialization that is improper, that violates a process norm. That does not follow once you accept the notion that indoctrination is in part what schools are about. The ultimate decisionmakers, the ultimate seats of sovereignty—state legislature, maybe statewide board of education, local school board—are not going to be making all the decisions, they are going to delegate. But there is nothing inconsistent with our normal theories of efficiency or political representation when we state that it's perfectly appropriate for the ultimate decisionmakers to come in on an *ad hoc, ex post facto* basis when the populace is really aroused, when they notice that there is something that violates their overall vague sense of socialization. They say, "Oh, no. Now that we see that you've done this and we have a socialization mission here and that violates our mission, we're going to come in *ad hoc, ex post facto,* and we'll stop that." If you concede to them the power to indoctrinate, it seems to me that you can't make them operate only according to more general forward-looking principles. That doesn't logically follow, once you make the concession about indoctrination. So I don't think that the idea Professor Yudof outlines for a process norm relating to this irrevocable delegation doctrine holds up. You're carrying it over from a rather different context when you're dealing with entitlements and with adjudicative rather than legislative types of decisions.

Much the same thing holds, I think, with the idea of structural due process. All the cases Professor Yudof cites are cases in which the courts have said that the state legislature, in its discretion, can place a premium on the local community as the unit of reference in decisionmaking. To impose localism rather than a statewide norm in the name of the Constitution is a very different matter, and there are other problems with the structural due process theory.

It is the same with his motivation theory. To an extent, I think what he is doing is invoking an idea that Gerry Gunther put forth some years ago, that once the legislature has articulated a value, you measure that against an efficiency standard. Are they really efficiently serving the value that they have articulated? Much of his motivational analysis is based on the premise that motivation is illicit if it's inconsistent with what the state board professes to be its mission. I think that doesn't necessarily apply in a lot of these cases. The state board may just change its role from censor to editor and be more direct, more open, about the kind of socialization that it's doing. So, in that sense, I'm not quite as optimistic as Mark is about whether these process norms will be very fruitful in evolving legal doctrine.

APPLYING THE FIRST AMENDMENT

There may be more to what I'm calling substantive norms. The big problem here is that we lack a theory of the grievance, what is it, really? Who is being harmed? How are they being harmed? Once we make the fundamental concession that schools, to some extent, are for the purpose of inculcating or socializing, and you can use the more pejorative words as well, does that completely explode our theory of the grievance? Because if we have no real sense, no points of reference, no benchmark, as to what it is that is wrong, how can we identify the First Amendment violation? Now, Mark suggests (it's more implicit in his paper) three different starting points or theories of agreement. One is what you might call the Meikeljohnian vision. That means what schools are about and what the Constitution requires that schools be about without regard to the political process is, at least in significant part, producing the Meikeljohnian self-governors. It means there is a kind of socialization process decreed by the Constitution that produces independent citizens prepared to take an active role in self-government. Now, it's interesting that Meikeljohn (who is cited all the time by the Supreme Court as God-like in stature in terms of just rhetoric) stressed the education component of the First Amendment as much as the free expression component. He said that if you're really thinking about what the First Amendment means, it means leaving them free to debate and express themselves. There's always been a problem with Meikeljohn. Lawyers read him and love him and then try to translate his soaring philosophical notions into workable doctrine and usually come up empty-handed.

In part, preparing people for self-government is carrying on a tradition, even if it means the civic cliches—in the tense moments we do invoke the founding fathers and call upon a kind of residual respect for these notions of liberty and so forth. But is also requires a kind of independence of thought and any curriculum which doesn't attempt to nurture independence of thought is failing to respond to the Meikeljohnian view of the First Amendment. In that sense, you can try to build doctrines from that.

A second starting point might be the public forum/marketplace of First Amendment values. Here you've got to deal with the objection based on the claim that schools are a special environment. In the general run of First Amendment disputes, special environments call for rather different kinds of analyses. You have to have a special kind of structuring of the market—for example, prisons, the military, perhaps even the broadcast medium. Many objections are that the schools are, in that sense, different. It may well be that broadcasting is the best analogy. Nonetheless, we still believe that there's something like a balance or a marketplace that has to be preserved in broadcasting. Some notions of freedom are important in thinking about these questions. If's not entirely that it's a closed environment and therefore the First Amendment is irrelevant, but it must be viewed in a somewhat different light. Perhaps you can try to do that in the school context, as well.

Should courts ever say that you have to have this particular textbook in the classroom to balance that textbook, and so on, then the notion of professional autonomy comes into play, though it's not often thought of in this particular context. One reason you grant professional autonomy is because you believe that's the best structure for creating the kind of marketplace which is the ultimate First Amendment value. The *Tornillo* decision regarding editorial freedom can probably be explained in that way.[12] These high school newspaper censorship cases might be explained. There's a certain kind of professional autonomy, editorial autonomy, which is your best strategy for achieving a kind of balanced marketplace. To carry that over into broader professional autonomy for librarians and specialists who make decisions about textbooks is a very big step. But looking at autonomy in that sense, I think, might be promising and that's how it would fit in.

Probably the most promising avenue is one that is seldom really articulated, although it's quite central to traditional First Amendment thinking. It is what I call the "proper role for government" model, or the "limited government" model. You can explain traditional First Amendment thought in terms of the simple proposition—sort of an eighteenth-century proposition—that we have a conception of the limits on government. It's built into the constitutional system that government can't do these sorts of things and can't use this as a reason or have this kind of motivation. We're not using motivation here as a basis for proving bad faith or failure to live up to previous commitments. Instead, it's that the government really can't have this kind of motivation or purpose in the constitutional scheme. We don't warmly respond to that kind of an idea in our constitutional system; we tend to emphasize rights and entitlements rather than any blueprint for government. But if eighteenth-century people who thought seriously about constitutional issues were to ask, "What will the courts tell us in the next two hundred years, what dimensions of political theory will be developed as a result of years of litigation?" I think many people would say, "We'll know a lot more about the legitimate ends of the state, what governments can legitimately do." Of course, we know very little about that as a result of our heritage of constitutional litigation. Instead, we know a lot more about individual entitlements and very little about what it is that government can invoke legitimately to advance its purposes.

If you look at a what lies behind First Amendment tradition, First Amendment thought, I think it is more this government-purpose side rather than the individual-claim or actual-impact-on-people side of it. Underlying the absolutism of Hugo Black and even Harry Kalven is the central proposition that government cannot have a censorial motivation or a censorial rationalization for what it is doing. It can achieve effects that resemble the same effects you would achieve under a censorial mission. But you actually can't have that as your rationale and motivation for government action. Also, by the prior restraint doctrine, there has always been a difficult theoretical problem. Why is it that prior restraints are special? Subsequent punishments can in many ways be just as hurtful to speakers, have just as much of a chilling effect, and so on. But, usually, behind a prior restraint is a kind of censorial or ideological judgment. It's an effort to keep an idea out of circulation, rather than to minimize certain kinds of costs that speech has for other kinds of reasons. It's an intrinsic aspect of First Amendment theory that government cannot be a censor—not because it will distort the marketplace of ideas, not because it will have some impact upon the kind of citizens that we develop, not because it will put the government in a position of being inconsistent with its own professed ideals, but simply because the First Amendment itself has as one of its core values that government cannot be a censor, cannot act out of that kind of motivation.

That doesn't even begin to solve the line-drawing problems, the infinitely difficult but merely practical problems. But I think it might be a more promising theoretical basis. There is one final touchpoint for this—I think it's very significant that the judges in *Cary* (the Tenth Circuit case)[13] and in *Zykan* (the Seventh Circuit case), even though they were basically rejecting claims, indicated that if this were part of an effort to establish orthodoxy, it would be a totally different case. There is something at the intuitive level which suggests that government's trying to impose an orthodoxy violates the First Amendment. We can't have governments doing that. It reflects a strong intuition in judges who aren't otherwise reaching out to embrace these kinds of claims, that at some point government is going beyond its own mandate when it strives to impose an orthodoxy. That's the starting point for developing a First Amendment doctrine. And we should work hard on the line-drawing problems starting from there.

INCULCATION VERSUS INDOCTRINATION

Mr. Van Alstyne:

I would like to turn to an area of the subject we've not touched on, and that is the specific difficulty in public library book selection and removal. Very little that I've listened to seems terribly helpful with that different branch of the problem on book control and selection. Despite my criticism of Mark Yudof's paper, there is a powerful merit in several of his observations. The principal one which he caught in his forensic presentation is a kind of modification of his notion of delegation—that is, the safety of the First Amendment through balkanization of public education. Some of his remarks may have seemed theoretically at odds with John Stuart Mill's essay on liberty, but that's not the case. You may recall that in Mill's essay he makes an exception with regard to all else that he writes about the autonomy of human beings to make their own discreet decisions as they themselves judge best to their own satisfaction and welfare. He makes an exception of children on exactly the same ground, albeit not to the same extent as those who have been fairly adjudicated mentally incompetent, that they are not yet ready for that exercise of autonomy. And I take it that it is part of Mill's essay on liberty to suggest that the general task of government with regard to children is not to make democracy safe for children, but rather to make children safe for democracy.

One way to make democracy safe for those who are "children," though they're over the age of twenty-one, is by following a kind of Skinnerian technique of such reflexive conditioning that, though immature adults, they are so automatically controlled by all that has gone before that their conduct will be born reliable and safe. They lack critical capacities to do things which strike other people as problematic if not downright dangerous. The task, therefore, of public education, according to this view, is to raise older children by this process of skillful inculcation.

But I thought that the Millian approach was very different from this. It is to recognize the gradual states of maturation in infancy for what they are; and to cultivate each person's critical skills, which, once they are developed at appropriate and differential ages, then make people quite safe to align with virtually any doctrine of their own choosing.

That for me is a very profound difference. It explains the intelligibility of some decisions, for instance, that look ideologically partisan, but may in fact simply represent a good faith judgment that this material is premature at this particular age. It is like the controversy that plagues public libraries as to whether books that teach how to make a gun ought necessarily be available to all, or only to some adults under certain conditions. Some of the controversy on book selection and course preparation material for different age groups studying sex hygiene is of the same kind. It is not entirely ideological. It is partly a kind of Millian concern that the teaching materials are premature in terms of the skills they present and the maturation of the person capable of handling it. From my own point of view, it is at least ideologically indifferent and does not deserve nearly the same kind of harsh criticism that is appropriately made of governmental invasion of the systematic organization of classrooms for purposes of raising a safe, infantile, adult population. One way of going about this is merely to rest on balkanization.

There's great wisdom in that. As long as there are other schools operating in this field that teach a contrasting point of view, sooner or later in the greater diversity of the national ideological marketplace, it will all sort itself out. In terms of national policies, there will be a larger competitive ideological marketplace where those ideas will compete for their favor one way or another. Thus the hesitation and reservation many of us had in the mere establishment of a federal department of education, not because of misgivings about who currently superintends it, but because insofar as we nationalize and homogenize an entire educational system, we lose some of the values of diversity.

But I agree with the doctrine that First Amendment purposes are significantly served through all varieties of strategies. The nation may not suffer because the centers of ideology will ultimately have to compete in a larger national marketplace. But human beings suffer individually insofar as they are crippled by the insufficiency of being nurtured without the evolution of critical skills to cope with ideas. They will be children at large in a democracy. The current permissive *dicta* by the Supreme Court notwithstanding, I think it's a fundamental error to give up trying to separate the teaching of skills, without which people may not be able to cope at all, and the systematic inculcation of an uncritical point of view on any of these matters.

ENCOURAGING DIVERSITY

Mr. Yudof:

Many of the criticisms are well taken, but let me just comment on some. As I neared the end of my paper, I felt a growing despair. How was I going to advise this group of litigators that there is no hope? I was groping around for a notion that perhaps you could show this illicit motivation to censor, to indoctrinate, that that standing by itself would be enough. And I was relying upon Dworkin's theories about racial discrimination—that even though you might have neighborhood schools anyhow, why you might want integration, because the process is corrupted by racial prejudice. If you could show that the process was corrupted by this effort to censor, to get the ideas out of the schools, and not good faith judgments about educating children, then who cares if exactly the same result could have been accomplished through some other mode of thinking? I did not consider the motivation theory to be sustainable under process analysis. It was that government is not supposed to act out of these motives, period.

The other thing is that professional editorial autonomy really does fit in with the delegation notion. That is, it's no easier to fit it in under a public forum or marketplace of ideas theory. If you strengthen the professional autonomy, you are consistent with perhaps all three of the underlying types of value structures that we talked about. Those are the self-controlled citizen, the marketplace of ideas, and an appropriate limitation of government control and substantive limitation.

Norman Dorsen:

This is really a hard issue. It seems to me that we're groping again for a value, on the substantive side, initially—a value that we think is both defensible and translatable into usable legal doctrine. The value we're most concerned about is diversity/nonorthodoxy. We're trying to find a way to avoid imposition of orthodoxy by the government or, conversely, to encourage diversity and to permit access to different ideas by the pupils or students.

The paradox is that there are two entirely inconsistent ways of reaching that goal. One way is to permit autonomous local groups to make their decisions free of any centralizing authority. Bill Van Alstyne's point was that in the long run, past countless school boards everywhere, all kinds of diverse ideas will be heard and seen and the students will get access to them. The difficulty is that there may not be diversity because an orthodoxy will be imposed within the unit. And how do you cure that? You cure it by having the alternative, a centralizing body, namely the federal courts, ultimately imposing diversity by impeding a local unit's decisions to impose orthodoxy. The trouble with that is that once you get a centralizing authority in the name of government imposing diversity, it can impose orthodoxy in the guise of diversity. It can be making decisions which, while nominally seeking variety, will ultimately represent the views of five people, namely a majority of the Supreme Court of the United States. And who is appointing those five people? That is the ultimate problem.

Now, for a theory. In the ACLU's brief in the *Pentagon Papers* case,[14] we spelled out an argument that was adopted, in fact, by one Justice of the Court, Justice Marshall. Among other arguments we made was that the government had no legislative authority to seek an injunction in cases of this kind. The government's answer was that it had an inherent power.

Another type of argument is a *Kent* v. *Dulles*[15] argument—that before the government, the Secretary of State, can deny somebody a passport (which, of course, interferes with travel), the reason has to be spelled out with clarity. It was held in that case, even though it was *dicta* by Douglas, that there was a consitutional liberty of travel. That was basically a delegation case, finding there was no authority in the Secretary of State.

How does all this apply here? Perhaps we could come to a theory of orthodoxy, if our object is to prevent government imposition of orthodoxy. If a court could find that in certain circumstances action by government at any level threatened to impose orthodoxy on a school system or a library, you could possibly argue that you'd need a clear legislative mandate to do that. Because of the interferences with freedom to read or to learn diverse ideas, you would need a clear and explicit legislative directive authorizing the imposition of this orthodoxy. In the absence of that, the action would be invalid and remanded in effect the way *Kent v. Dulles* remanded the passport case to Congress which, subsequently, never explicitly authorized any imposition of these passport controls.

The second, more far-reaching alternative would be to find an imposition of orthodoxy by the government that in itself is a violation of a constitutional right. The imposition of orthodoxy may be analogous to the right to know in a number of cases. I realize that doctrine has had its limitations, very severe limitations. Nevertheless, we have some doctrine that could support a judicial finding. One book or another book wouldn't do it; you would have to have some kind of pattern. If you could show that that pattern really was an attempt to impose orthodoxy, that would be a violation related to academic freedom, related to right to know, and related to freedom of access to diverse intellectual materials within the school system.

Howard Besser:

It's obvious that we're all taken with the concept of power in the local community, or balkanization, or avoiding orthodoxy— you can phrase it in different ways. We have this concern that both Professor Dorsen and Professor Van Alstyne recognize as the tyranny of the prevailing thought, the tyranny of the majority, as it were. They really knew what they wanted, these people who thought of the First Amendment. And I think that's part of the Meikeljohnian theory as well. It's this elusive search for the truth with a pluralistic approach. We're seeking access. We're seeking a widening so that people can be educated and presumably be better citizens. The problem of placing the power in the local community is the assumption that the local community is somehow educated or qualified enough to make those kinds of judgments. That's a troublesome thing. I realize it is somewhat destructive of our whole democratic ideal and democratic process, and that's something we have never really grappled with.

I'm troubled by this comment about the right to know in Professor Yudof's paper. "If students have a right to know, then they should have a constitutional right to demand courses in public schools that are not offered for financial or other reasons." I think that conclusion does not follow, that syllogism does not lie.

Mr. Yudof:

That was my point. All the cases that I could find involved willing speakers, and the notion that the school board would say, "We don't want to tell you," and then the student would say, "But I want to know"—that's the reason I felt that the *Virginia Pharmacy* case[16] and the prison cases and all really were not applicable. In this context, if one asserted a right to know, one would have to find the willing speaker. Maybe you could do that because maybe you could point to the teacher's academic freedom. There may be circumstances where that's true, but the core notion of the school board declining to offer a course about women in literature, when someone contends that he or she has a right to know about women in literature, is not a case that can be decided under the *Virginia Pharmacy* standard; it just doesn't fit.

THE ROLE OF THE SCHOOLS

Ira Glasser:

What we've done is leap to strategy questions without resolving our goals. We keep raising analytic problems and internal contradictions and paradoxes, all of which flow from our failure to confront the problem and to answer the question, What do we want the schools to be for? Never mind our different views of what schools are, or what they were intended to be, or what other people think they are with respect to indoctrination and the definition of information or education. But what do we want them to be in First Amendment terms? What do we think is the right thing? Who defines these questions and gives the answers? Is it the community? What community? Are we going to get into obscenity law questions about the larger community, the smaller community? Our school systems were as balkanized, maybe more balkanized, in the 1950s than they are now; and there was a greater pall of orthodoxy then, because there wasn't very much variation from balkan state to balkan state among the 26,000 school districts. There were good social reasons for that, and those social reasons have now changed. All this turmoil over books in the schools is the most hopeful thing when you consider that you could not even have dreamed of those kinds of fights thirty years ago. Then you had the balkanization and the delegation of authority, but you didn't have any censorship. Nobody was circulating lists—I mean there were lists with George Orwell and things like that, but you didn't even reach that question in most places—nothing controversial was discussed and nobody assumed that it ever would be.

In public school education it was just a question of time served until you got out. And if you learned anything, you learned it somewhere else. You learned it when you got to college or in some other way. Now what has happened is very different. All the turmoil and all the openness encouraged by television, and even more so by cable television, will sweep aside a lot of these problems and put them in a very different context. It is now impossible for the censors to achieve their results, even if they succeed in getting a book out of a local school. The child who doesn't get to read *One Flew over the Cuckoo's Nest* in the school, thanks to the controversy, will buy it in paperback or see it in the movies. Or he may wait until his parents leave and watch it on cable television. When my eleven-year-old joined in the conversation at dinner by saying that *The Tin Drum*—an R-rated movie—didn't seem so explicitly sexual to her, I asked her, "How would you know what was explicitly sexual?" And my thirteen-year-old child said, "Well, it's suggestive." And I said, "Suggestive of what?" Something has happened you see. While we all discuss what these children should know and be exposed to, they are exposed, regardless of these fine distinctions and court resolutions. We're merely jockeying about the positions of these boats on a sea that has moved very far from where it once was.

In this time of cultural transition, when we're dealing with the symptomatic reactions to these changes, we may have to concentrate on preserving the doctrinal solidity of the First Amendment so that we don't get involved in putting forth propositions which have a lot of overbroad and unintended effects. This is a double-edged sword that we're using. Diversity may mean including a view that's currently excluded. Our opponents are using these libertarian arguments and I am not sure that any of us has the final answer to that.

We need to reconsider what, in terms of the First Amendment, we are trying to preserve during this difficult cultural time, when people are reacting to very rapid change of social mores by seeking to control that which they can no longer control. Perhaps our effort should be to preserve the First Amendment so that when that time passes, we will not have unintentionally created doctrines that will damage the very ends we want the First Amendment to protect. We're really dealing with footnotes to a larger problem when we discuss strategies to achieve results that we're not at all clear about.

STRATEGIES FOR LITIGATION

Judith Krug:

The reality for this session is that librarians and teachers are human beings—something very important to remember as we go into litigation strategy. We have to preserve our people, especially those people who have the guts and the backbone and the *chutzpa*, if you will, to stand up and fight. Because when the pressures come, our people are totally isolated; the community joins against them. And sometimes the only supports that they have are the associations that are represented at this conference today. As litigators, you are part of that network to whom we do turn as the occasions arise. But even before that, there are certain strategies that can be utilized, reviewed, and put into a working order that will indeed help us.

There are two strategies that the Freedom to Read Foundation has been promoting since its inception in 1969. The first one Professor Yudof covered in his paper, and that is "procedures"—the saving element. We are attempting to convince all of our people to abide by the procedures that have been adopted in theory by the school boards and by the boards of trustees of public libraries. Some of the most important procedures are material selection statements, which delineate the requirements that will be reviewed in selection of the specific materials for library collections in schools and public libraries and, to a large extent, detail the kinds of materials that are used in the classroom. That is one way that we exercise some control over the selection procedure.

The second thing that the Freedom to Read Foundation has been attempting to do is to take the "sex" out of censorship. We try to move the pressure away from the individual librarian, in our case, or the individual teacher, and put the book on trial, or the magazine, or the film, through *in rem* civil proceedings. If we take the "sex" out of censorship—that is, the ability to, in effect, nail a human being to the wall—we may indeed cool off the would-be censors. It becomes extremely time-consuming, and really not terribly exciting, to take every piece of material, to follow the adopted procedure, and then, eventually, to get to court. There is only so much time, money, and energy that would-be censors want to devote to this process. We may in this way lose a few of the battles, but we're going to have something to stand on and eventually, hopefully, win the war.

James Klenk:

What I've heard today from the law professors and litigating lawyers confirms the advice I give clients—that is, you shouldn't litigate unless you have the right case, because the law in this area is very tough. We're having a hard time finding a coherent legal theory here. What win these cases are facts. So we have to find good facts. We have to take measures short of litigation wherever possible. At the Freedom to Read Foundation, we advocate having procedures and following them. This puts roadblocks in people's paths and buys you time— maybe they'll trip up on something, and you can use that in your litigation. I'm just amazed that we haven't come up with a legal theory yet, but maybe the answer is that it will take time to evolve a coherent theory.

Alan Levine:

Let's discuss libraries versus curriculum legal theory. We litigated *Presidents Council*[17] on the assumption that it presented a rather straightforward First Amendment violation. The state had removed a book from the library and therefore, to some extent, had inhibited First Amendment values. We suggested that the state was obliged then to come up with some justification. There was no justification in the record in that case and therefore we said to the court, "We should prevail." The Second Circuit rejected that. They talked about "book tenure" theory, in that once a book was there it didn't get tenure and so there's no difference between removal of a book and acquisition of a book. I continue to believe there is and, indeed, *Minarcini*[18] suggests that the library case presents more traditional First Amendment issues than does the curriculum case. I think it's important for litigators to remember that. In the Second Circuit, it didn't help us very much when it came to *Pico* because there was *Presidents Council* staring us in the face. But *Minarcini* and cases elsewhere have explored whatever justification it is that the state advances for their action, and I think it's important to focus on that justification.

That suggests maybe we're looking to their motivation, and we have to. That gets to the issue of facts. It is important to litigate facts, but it's important to avoid certain facts. One of the things that happened in *Presidents Council* is that we obtained affidavits from experts who said the books in question were perfectly appropriate for junior high school students. Besides the experts, we had all the rating services and school library rating services. They deemed *Down These Mean Streets* an appropriate book. The defendants brought in psychologists and psychiatrists with respectable credentials who said no, that twelve- and thirteen-year-olds are sexually immature; they are in transition and this book will stunt their sexual growth and cause them social problems. That was a risk that we had in mind in *Pico*. It was a risk that was made more real to us by a successor case in the Second Circuit, *Trachtman v. Anker*,[19] in which a group of students in a high school sought to distribute a sex education survey. It was a rather benign undertaking. But either the school board or the superintendent was offended and it went to the New York City school board. They upheld the ban, we litigated it, and the district court split the difference with us. They said that the sex survey could be distributed to eleventh and twelfth graders, but not ninth and tenth graders. Expert opinion was relied on both in the district court and then, ultimately, in the Second Circuit which reversed the district court and said no, there was the fear here of an emotional disruption and therefore a state interest.

When you get to *Island Trees*, the issue is whether to litigate the books. It was clear that at least in the Second Circuit you incur trouble if you litigate the books. Sure, *The Fixer* is a National Book Award winner and Vonnegut's *Slaughterhouse-Five* is beyond reproach. You might win on a few books, but there was a real danger that you could lose on seven or eight of the others. In Judge Mansfield's dissent in *Pico*, you see that he focused on all these excerpts from the books. You can have reams of vulgarity from all of these books. If you deem that an appropriate standard and get some psychologists or psychiatrists to predict problems for adolescents thereby, then you're going to lose that case. You're certainly going to lose it in the Second Circuit.

In the Second Circuit, and I think elsewhere, you want to litigate facts. You want to litigate the censors as much as possible. And that's what we did in *Island Trees*. Our facts were derived from finding out who the censors were and what they knew about the books. It turned out they knew very little about the books. The kind of things they said about the books when quoted in the Second Circuit, at least in the two favorable opinions, made them look silly. They said things about vulgarity, but they also said that the works contained very explicit political statements. There were comments about Malcolm X, one of whose essays appeared in one of these books, and comments about Eldridge Cleaver. Then, in depositions they commented on a book called *A Hero Ain't Nothin' but a Sandwich* in which one of the characters identified George Washington as a slaveholder. In the deposition, a school board member opined that that was anti-American and inappropriate for schoolbooks to teach. By careful inquiry, that kind of statement will emerge.

We have to cope with the issue of vulgarity. We have a problem if we concede that the only issue that violates the First Amendment, the only kind of censorship, the only kind of actionable removal or ban or prohibition is one that is explicitly political. You know, in *Island Trees*, we may still win—even though now the opposite side sprinkles the record with its concern about vulgarity—because there's so much political stuff in the case. But they're going to learn their lesson the next time.

One can certainly look at these books and say that the problem is vulgarity, if that is a legitimate basis for censorship. Banning a book because it contains some four-letter words is contrary to the First Amendment. Certainly the obscenity cases teach us that. To concede to a school board the power to ban books because they contain vulgarity is really to concede to them a broad political power. It would give them the power to ban much of what is considered great in twentieth-century American literature. There must be an ideological theme that is incorporated in a ban of vulgarity. This is one of the issues that has to be addressed here. Judge Newman, who expresses concern about vulgarity, says that the power of school boards to ban vulgarity is not without limit, that there are First Amendment limitations upon that right of a school board.

Frank Parker:

Do you, as a litigator, see a danger in having social science testimony as to the educational appropriateness of the book, knowing that there will be rebuttal evidence? And then the judge says that reasonable social scientists can disagree. Therefore, we defer to the board. It's the same problem I've had in desegregation suits where someone says a particular type of school injures or advances the progress of blacks. And another set of professional expert witnesses is summoned and says the opposite. Then there's a tendency to say this is an educational question about which educators or psychologists sincerely differ. It seems to me that by putting on the evidence in the first place, you may have given away part of the game. Is that your view?

Alan Levine:

That certainly was the concern when we came to *Island Trees*. *Presidents Council* caused concern. In essence what the court said in both cases was—it was their First Amendment analysis—that they really saw themselves as reviewing an administrative determination which they considered to be reasonable. We argued that the board had to have a compelling interest which hadn't been met there. But as long as the record provides a handle for the school board to support itself, a handle better than the one they can come up with on their own, then it is better to leave experts out of it.

Frank Parker:

In *Loewen,* the Mississippi history text litigation, we had a lot of historians come in and testify that our book was good and the other book was bad. They were worried that this might create an issue. The defendants were not able to get one historian to testify that our book should not have been accepted by the state authorities. They got a witness list of about five or six historians and we called some of them and they told us, "No, I'm not going to say that your book should have been banned, that it should not have been put on the list." They were not able to get a single historian. Now, I think in the state of Mississippi, with twenty of them on the state payroll, that was really unbelievable.

Alan Levine:

They should have come to New York. There would have been plenty of them.

Frank Parker:

Historians, at least in Mississippi, really believe in the First Amendment.

Henry Kaufman:

Jonathan Shapiro, you did a lot of affidavit work testifying on literary merit in the *Chelsea* case, did you not?

Jonathan Shapiro:

Yes. You always run the risk, whether you put on expert testimony or not, that the other side will come in and put on expert testimony to the effect that the removed material is inappropriate. So I'm not sure that you're giving up anything by opening the door. In fact, if you can put on credible enough expert testimony, you may so embarrass the opposition that they will not be able to come forward with expert testimony themselves. And, as Henry points out, in the *Chelsea* case we spent a considerable amount of time putting on expert testimony as to the appropriateness of this particular anthology of poetry and prose as a tool for teaching English. We had a fairly well-known professor from Boston University who was an expert on the teaching of high school teachers. And he testified to that effect. We also had the dean of the SUNY School of Library Science testify to the appropriateness of the particular book in the library. The result was that the school board did come up with someone whom they portrayed as an expert. It turned out that he was a math teacher who had taught English briefly twenty-five years before at the junior high school level. And that was the only person they secured who would testify that, in his opinion, the book was in any way inappropriate. The use of expert testimony to establish some kind of educational norm is awfully important. You can show that the defendants are simply being arbitrary, in the almost traditional due process analysis sense. You don't even have to get to some of the more thorny First Amendment problems if you can show that the state is acting arbitrarily and that it affects an important interest of citizens. That's unconstitutional.

To the extent that the state is acting to censor, to suppress ideas, the argument is that you made a *prima facie* case simply by showing that the state took that action. The burden is then shifted to the defendants to show compelling interest or, as in the *Chelsea* case in which the court required the showing of a substantial and important state interest akin to the interest in *Tinker*,[20] disruption and so forth. Once you get that far, you've almost won the case. Even if the state then comes back with a reason, as they did in *Pico*, to suggest that something is inappropriate or educationally wrong, you can show that the basis for their action is a pretext in the sense that: (1) they didn't make an educational decision in the first place, rather it was the conservatives or Moral Majority who published the list of books; and (2) there are other books in the library containing the selfsame language about which they had known for years and had never done anything (which is what you'll find in most libraries). In the *Chelsea* case, they took the position that the vulgar words themselves were the problem, but then they had to deal with the fact that there were dozens of other books in the library with the same words and that their reason was obviously a pretext, which then still wins you the case.

Henry Kaufman:

Is there case law here, or is the net effect of the discussion that there's nothing, and we've got to start from scratch and fight about facts that may or may not be persuasive to the courts?

Mr. Van Alstyne:

The trouble isn't the lack of case law. In a sense, we're engulfed by it. And much of it is very ill advised. The statements by some courts are so unhelpful that we scarcely dare repair to it. However, there are some additional useful case analogies. There's an analogy to other kinds of cases not involving schools or libraries. An excellent analogy that cuts both ways, as well, is the Supreme Court's decision in the *Pacifica Foundation* case.[21] Those of you who may not recall it by name will surely recall it by its facts. That's the case involving a record cut by George Carlin wonderfully entitled "Seven Dirty Words You Can't Say on Television." Well, it turns out that you can't say them on radio either because an FM station in San Francisco presumed to play it—or was it New York?

That case came out badly in one way. It was rationalized as a time, place, and manner control. There are alternative access points to the same record, such as record stores. But, surprisingly, the case may be helpful. A lot of doctrine can be applied to many of these school library cases. It's not the classroom (where the student is more captive), it's merely the library. It's a place of access. Even on profanity or vulgarity, if you translate *Pacifica Foundation* into that environment, it's a very difficult kind of problem. The *Pacifica* case would be even more like some of these more difficult cases if, in *Pacifica*, the radio licensee had not complained but acquiesced. If they had simply received the complaint forwarded to them by the FCC and decided, "Well, it's better to switch than to fight. We may very well lose, and in any case, it's a lot of money." The question of a practical nature that joins with the theoretical question on time, place, and manner, and ultimate censorship, then, is who has standing? Imagine the *Pacifica* case brought by anyone other than the licensee. Who would it be?

Some random adult who might have heard George Carlin's "Seven Dirty Words" but for the acquiescence of the FM station? It's a very hard case practically. It's harder theoretically because the issue that is presented is made diffuse.

Contrary to a suggestion offered earlier, intended to protect scupulous people in their jobs, we may need to enlarge a theory to find a suitable party to effectuate standing in a way more equivalent to *Pacifica Foundation*. This would get us standing when we can't find a palpably injured party but merely have this sense of indirect injury to a much larger body politic by the blanking out of particular books or other phenomena. In some of these instances, librarians may be pivotal people to bring the claim.

They borrow third-party standing. They represent everyone else, as well, but like the FM radio station, they present a claim of their own: a librarian's "professional" First Amendment freedom. It is cognate to an academician's freedom—academic freedom in the narrow sense, deference owed to the professional instructor with regard to that person's discretion to include or exclude certain materials in the classroom. That has been successfully litigated in some cases which would otherwise have failed. The teacher makes the decision, on the presumption of entitlement, that the courts and school boards should defer to his or her discretion. School boards must then overcome the rebuttable presumption of professional integrity in that decision. The court may maintain its posture of deference by saying it is not for courts to say. It is in the first instance for the academician to say. And unless the board can come up with convincing evidence that *that* decision by the academician was professionally inappropriate, then the court defers by saying the teacher wins. Deference is still maintained because you have inserted a new party with its own standing and special claim.

Try to enlarge upon the thin but promising line of cases asserting an independent academician's claim to professional discretion of a defensible kind against contrary directives by school authorities or others. Try to work toward some kind of equivalent professional freedom with regard to the librarian who monitors the integrity of the system when the removal of books is sought.

There are hazards. In most cases where academic freedom wins, the academician involved leaves shortly thereafter. We all know that successful cases have had heavy personal casualties. Attorneys have to face the poignancy of those dilemmas when they encourage the registering of that special kind of standing. But if you want additional theory analogously supported in established areas of law and something practical to fill these gaps, this is one additional avenue to consider.

Unidentified Speaker:

In looking for more familiar doctrines that might be relevant, it is interesting that no one has mentioned the case of *Bantam Books, Inc.* v. *Sullivan.*[22] In that case, there was an informal citizens' group which went around informing booksellers of disfavored books and having a considerable intimidating effect on many booksellers. The Supreme Court, early on in its development of the expanse of First Amendment doctrine, held that that was a prior restraint. That phenomenon seems not to have seen litigation or to have been terribly important in the particular areas we've been discussing. That may be a testimonial to the strength and independence of the professionals we've discussed, who are less easily intimidated by that kind of community pressure than are commercial booksellers. But the time may come when informal intimidation looms larger in affecting curricular decisions and decisions about what will be stocked and removed from school libraries. It will then be very important to develop legal doctrine dealing with such technical matters as standing and establishing threshold violations based on that *Bantam Books* analogy.

Henry Kaufman:

Are you suggesting that publishers should attempt to develop their own standing in this context?

Unidentified Speaker:

Well, to some extent. Just to build on that, there's another case analogy that we may not have previously thought out. There's the so-called eyebrow-lifting case of the FCC regarding the "family viewing" hour.[23] The FCC never promulgated a specific rule; rather, the FCC chairman did some jawboning with the broadcasters, and they collegially agreed to adopt the rule that had merely been tentatively suggested.

Henry Kaufman:

Wasn't that reversed on appeal?

Unidentified Speaker:

But not on that point. So it's a nice carry forward of the *Bantam Book* technique suggesting an appropriate point to test the proposition that's at hand. Perhaps the publishers will be able to assert some degree of standing of their own in that kind of "intimidation" proceeding.

Unidentified Speaker:

When you have to present claims of this sort, not in terms of the student's welfare or of the audience, but rather in terms of the claims of the publishers to make a profit or to distribute their product, or, alternatively, in terms of notions of professional autonomy, it becomes much more difficult to persuade wavering judges. I saw this vividly in working extensively on the news reporter's privilege issue. Whenever the right of the newspaper reporter to practice his or her profession was raised, there was resistance in many quarters to that concept. You had to talk about the right of the newspaper-reading public to get a richer fare. It's unfortunate but we are forced to argue the cases and think about them in terms of publishers' rights, not professionals' rights.

Unidentified Speaker:

There's another aspect of the *Pacifica* case opinion which I find troubling and that is that the seven words involved in the case were not by anyone's account obscene insofar as obscenity is applied to an adult audience. The court was quite clear that the words might have been vulgar but not obscene. Nevertheless, the court thought it appropriate for a governmental body to threaten to cancel the license of a private station if it continued to permit broadcast of those nonobscene words even if the possible audience of children would not be a captive audience. That suggests that the same justices who voted in the majority on *Pacifica* would rule that school boards can prohibit that kind of language in the schools even if it is not obscene—another pessimistic note.

Alan Levine:

There is one theoretical, doctrinal handle that applies to schools that doesn't apply to the world out there. And that is academic freedom. If it means something, it means less that professionals have certain rights that other professionals don't have, than it does that it's for students. Students are affected by the pall of orthodoxy in the way that a listener could never seriously argue in the *Pacifica* case that he or she was affected. I think that gives a doctrinal handle that doesn't lead me to say that students have the right to control the curriculum— clearly they don't—but that they do have an academic freedom or right, although somewhat vague, tied up in this notion

of pall of orthodoxy, which recurs throughout the *Pico* opinion. And if we go back to trial in that case, and in any other
cases, that's what courts are going to be looking for.

Mr. Yudof:

I believe deeply in these autonomous citizens, who learn about
language and culture and about our literary traditions and the
like, but who also can step out of it, criticize our institutions,
and grow into adults who will cast, within any normal sense,
voluntary preferences in the political processes. What sort of
teacher accomplishes that? Well, it's the outstanding teacher
who is able to tell the students simultaneously, "These are our
traditions, but we don't have to retain them forever; there
may be some problems with them. You should at least think
about them critically." We object to orthodoxy because it can
contract the mind, but how do we know it when we see it?
Lots of things contract the mind. If you could identify the
orthodoxy, then you'd be on your way to succeeding in some
of these cases.

Alan Levine:

What Judge Newman says we're to prove when we go back
to trial, notwithstanding that some of us thought we had
proved it when we came around to the Second Circuit the first
time, is essentially political orthodoxy, or at least orthodoxy
of ideas. What he really demands proof about is that the
school board here was not content neutral—it's obvious the
school board is never content neutral, but there were disfavored ideas here. Of course, most of the academic freedom
cases in which "pall of orthodoxy" is discussed clearly involve
ideas; they're mostly the loyalty oath cases. In *Island Trees*, I
think we're likely to be able to do it because the record is so
full of it. The question is, Are you then going to be able to
do it in other cases when they come up with this pretext?
They're not going to say ideas; they're generally going to say
words. That's one handle. Also, when you look at the kinds
of books that are gathered together for banning, there's some
similarity. They're mostly political books; they're mostly by
black writers, or writers who are writing about ghetto life. It's
an argument we made in *Presidents Council*, but the court did
not buy it.

Henry Kaufman:

Ann is going to tell us how she got summary judgment in the
Brautigan[24] case.

Ann Brick:

> *Brautigan* is a library case and it seems to me that the kind of
> orthodoxy Professor Yudof talked about was involved in the
> *Brautigan* case. Involved were books that somebody, eight
> years ago, thought were just fine for the library. Theoretically,
> it could have been a different school board with different
> political ideas. In fact, it was a teacher who bought the books.
> Nobody really cared and everything was fine until the princi-
> pal suspected it was sex education. The argument that had
> some persuasive value—really a "why not?" argument when
> you're dealing with the school library—is what is the reason
> for removing books except for fear of exposing the students
> to ideas? In this case, they argued very strenuously that they
> didn't like the language or the explicit sexual references. But
> it's almost a "so what?" argument because you don't have a
> captive audience. In First Amendment terms, what good rea-
> son is there for denying access to as broad a range of books
> as possible, assuming you're not running out of space in the
> library or the books are not worn out?

Anthony Schulte:

> The great majority of incidents, whether or not they get to be
> litigated, are, in fact, library incidents. The great majority of
> those, according to what we've seen in the survey Michelle
> Kamhi spoke about, are not about political content but are,
> in fact, about sexual description through what is defined as
> either objectionable language or too explicit depiction. The
> best defense may be selection procedures and responses to
> challenges so that the community will not be vulnerable to
> outside organizations saying, "Do you know what's going on
> in your community, Mr. Smith? Please send ten dollars to the
> Moral Majority and we'll help tell you what's going on in your
> community." Really, we're dealing mostly with librarians who
> are being attacked for selections in their collections, or teach-
> ers who simply recommend a list from which a student can
> choose books—nonobscene constitutionally—that deal with
> either sex or vulgarity in one way or another. That's really the
> question.

Unidentified Speaker:

> I would like to comment on the practical impact of censorship
> in the classroom. I am told that in Warsaw, Indiana, children
> started to think that the speakers in the room for public ad-
> dresses were really there for the purpose of listening to their
> discussions. Lo and behold, when some teacher asked a ques-

tion, the response was, "Well, I don't know if I can answer that; I'll have to wait until tomorrow until I can discover *[sic]* it." And these kinds of things seem to me to have an effect on the process of thought.

Schoolbook Censorship Litigation: A Litigator's Overview

Floyd Abrams

Once upon a time, when I was in my first year of law school, an incident occurred in my Contracts class which became burned indelibly in my otherwise none-too-clear memory. A student was called upon to summarize a case by our heavily Germanically accented professor. The student paused for a moment, as if debating whether or not to attempt to bluff it. Then, with a weary voice, he responded that he was not prepared since he had not read the case. The admission made, the student appeared to relax a bit as if the worst was over. But it hardly was. Our professor smiled genially at him and said something that I now recall sounding like "Zat is goot. From you, ve get ze fresh approach. Read the case now and then zummarize it for us."

Of course, the fresh approach offered by the student was a clumsy and faltering one—albeit one which compelled the attention (and sympathy) of the other students. What I offer you now is another somewhat similar fresh approach, that of one who is conversant with First Amendment law, who has (unlike my classmate) read the cases—but who has not been active and, until recently, at all knowledgeable in the schoolbook censorship area.[1] I present to you a melange of views reached after reading and rereading the cases decided in the field and (in most cases) the pleadings and records of those cases. I start with the complaint, move on to discovery, and then venture a few broader thoughts on the field.

THOUGHTS ON THE COMPLAINT

My first suggestions are ones which I would offer regarding the drafting of any complaint that I believed would likely be met with a motion to dismiss. It may be banal but it is surely essential to assure yourself that (a) proper parties commence the action and (b) the complaint itself states enough facts and articulates enough in the way of legal theory to allow the combat on a motion to dismiss to proceed on terms most favorable to the plaintiff.

As regards standing, you should plainly include students among your plaintiffs in any case involving schoolbook censorship if you are able to. They, more than anyone, clearly have standing, and if they are included as plaintiffs, there is likely to be less difficulty with respect to the standing of other plaintiffs. As a tactical matter, as well, the inclusion of students as plaintiffs is helpful in presenting the case to the court in its most appealing fashion. Also useful as plaintiffs, but less essential, are teachers (who have some rights of their own),[2] and a school librarian, if possible. I do not strenuously oppose the inclusion of others; but the inclusion of parents suing on their own behalf adds little to the case and may lead to a successful motion, at least as to them, based upon lack of standing.[3] Who needs it?

As regards the assertion of facts in the complaint, schoolbook censorship cases appear to lend themselves to "talking" complaints as opposed to reliance upon notice pleading. If you have a story to tell, the complaint is a first-rate place to start; if you do not, you should reconsider filing the complaint in the first place. A good example of a talking complaint is that in the *Right to Read* case involving the Chelsea, Massachusetts, high school.

To what extent should your complaint set forth—and flesh out— your legal theory? What your theory is will obviously be much affected by what part of the country you are in and what the governing law is there. Some cases from some parts of the country are extremely supportive of plaintiffs in schoolbook litigation, and in those places it might suffice simply to assert that the action of a school in removing (or not purchasing) a book violates the First Amendment. But why do this? Even in those areas, I think it advisable to set forth at least the theory previously approved (or not rejected) by the courts in the area—for example, that a decision to remove the books was based upon the individual political and social views of school board members, that a decision was intended to inculcate in the students certain political or social views of the school board, that the decision would have the effect of inculcating such views, and so forth. Of course, all these articulations of legal theory differ. I simply urge upon you that if you file your action in an area with decided case law, efforts should be made to conform your pleadings to the First Amendment law previously established in that area. And wherever you file the action, you should *talk* a bit in your complaint about the nature of and the improper legal consequences of the action of the school board. This should be done to the full extent the decided case law in your area allows—or does not preclude.

DISCOVERY

One reason why a particularly thorough complaint is important in a case of this sort is that such a pleading, containing numerous horrific factual contentions, should make it far easier to withstand a motion to dismiss. This should ensure you the opportunity for extensive discovery: of, for example, the (often irregular) procedure whereby the books were taken off the shelves; of the evaluations of the members of the school board (who often will not have read all sections of the books at issue); of the often incoherent, overtly groundless and even stupid explanations as to the reasons why those particular books (as opposed to others in the library which contain similar material) were selected.

The practitioner must, I submit, recognize that these cases do not raise the pure constitutional questions that some theoreticians prefer. Facts, and the ability to advantageously garner and organize the evidence, are no less significant in this legal area than any other.

A useful example may be found in the differing treatment by the Court of Appeals for the Second Circuit on the same day last fall of two theoretically similar cases.

In *Pico*[4] (the case where plaintiffs' claim that the board of education had unconstitutionally unshelved certain books in a Long Island school district was held to require a trial), the Second Circuit remanded the case to determine the actual effect of defendants' conduct on plaintiffs' exercise of their First Amendment rights. The *Pico* court relied on many facts already on the record in coming to its determination. The list of books to be censored was shown to have been made up by individuals having nothing whatsoever to do with that school district. The issue of the book banning, according to one of the defendants (an incumbent member of the board of education), had been a major one in the school board election campaign. In fact, an affidavit of that defendant did not help his cause by stating "nevertheless (or more probably because of this) the incumbent members were reelected." In *Pico* the presence of the election campaign and the procedural irregularities by which the banning was effected, in the court's view, warranted an inference that the welfare and education of the school children—the government interests involved—may not have been the true motivating concerns which led to the removal of the books.

In the other Second Circuit case, *Bicknell*,[5] facts evidencing such suppression of ideas by the authorities for political and ideological purposes were not offered and a school board's removal of what were claimed to be vulgar and obscene books was upheld.

Other types of facts which may be uncovered by discovery are of similar import. In some cases, depositions have shown the difficulty defendants have had in finding objectionable passages in the books at issue or in explaining why the books were removed. In *Pico*, for example, the court found "substantive confusion, not to say incoherence" as to such reasons. The difficulty of proof that the books had any harmful effects also can be brought out in deposition. For example, in *Wexner v. Anderson Union High School District Board of Trustees*, a very recent California state case involving the removal of five books by Richard Brautigan (in

: court granted student, teacher, and publisher plaintiffs' motion
iary judgment), the defendants at deposition were forced to
it the passages at issue which resulted in their removing the
re not at all harmful to the school children, but simply contained
views and tastes than those maintained by defendants. We
should all pray for one such deposition per case!

Depositions may also uncover that members of the school board,
even after voting to remove, had never read the books involved; or, as in
the Massachusetts case[6] where an anthology of writings by high school
children was removed because of one one-stanza poem, that the rest of
the anthology had never been read. Similarly, in a Mississippi case[7] the
fact that a number of raters, who chose to certify one textbook rather than
another (which gave a far more well-rounded view of Mississippi history),
gave no reasons at all on their evaluations for voting against plaintiffs'
textbook led the court to find that their explanation was a pretext for their
unjustified, and in that case racially discriminatory, decision.

One other type of fact which may be developed in discovery can be
used to a particular advantage in showing that the decision to ban certain
books was not because of the offensive passages in those books, but rather
because of objections to the social or political views espoused therein.
Questions as to the identity of many other books in the school library
containing the same vulgar words or offensive scenes is likely to result in
evidence that similarly objectionable books were not removed, thus raising an obvious argument that the reasons given for the banning were
pretextual. A case in point was *Salvail v. Nashua Board of Education*,[8]
where the board pulled copies of *Ms.* magazine from the school library
on the alleged grounds that it contained advertisements for vibrators and
contraceptives, and materials dealing with lesbianism and homosexuality
(as well as advertisements for a "pro-Communist newspaper," *The Guard-
ian*, advertisements suggesting trips to Cuba and solicitations for records
made by "known Communist folk singers"). The fact that similar materials were contained in other publications against which no removal proceedings were undertaken—*Redbook* and *Mademoiselle* contained articles
about the diaphragm, other contraceptives, and bust developers—easily
led the court to conclude that it was "the 'political' content of *Ms.*
magazine more than its sexual overtones that led to its arbitrary dis-
placement. Such a basis for removal of the publication is constitutionally
impermissible."

SOME REACTIONS TO FIRST AMENDMENT THEORY

The question which this last case, of course, raises is, Just what is
constitutionally impermissible? While that is, to some degree, beyond the
intended scope of this offering, let me suggest a few thoughts on the issue.

Thus far the courts have come to stunningly different and contradictory results. Certain courts, including federal district courts in New Hampshire and Massachusetts, the Court of Appeals for the Sixth Circuit, and a lower California state court, have concluded that it is "clear" that library books cannot be unshelved due solely to the political or social tastes of board members. On the other hand, the Second Circuit in *Presidents Council*,[9] *Pico* and *Bicknell* and the Seventh Circuit in *Zykan* v. *Warsaw Community School Corp.* have just as clearly held that such a motivation would not alone establish a constitutional violation.

The difference in results is the inevitable consequence of the differing First Amendment standards adopted by the different courts. Those courts which have been favorable to plaintiffs in finding that the personal taste of the board members is *not* a sufficient justification for removing books have done so on the grounds that the First Amendment interest to be protected is the right of the students to receive information which they and their teachers desire them to have—a "right to receive" information and ideas formulation recognized by the Supreme Court most forcefully in *Virginia State Board of Pharmacy* v. *Virginia Citizens Consumer Council, Inc.*[10] In that case, Mr. Justice Blackmun declared that where a speaker exists, "the protection afforded is to the communication, to its source and to its recipients both."

This sort of First Amendment interest is far easier to prove violated than the sort of First Amendment protection set forth in *Pico* where the Court of Appeals for the Second Circuit remanded the case for trial to inquire as to whether, in the removal of the books in question, there was the sort of "clearly defined, school-wide action that carries with it the potential for impermissible suppression of ideas." The requirement of proof of the actual suppression of ideas is a far more difficult standard to meet than proving that students have simply been blocked from receiving information.

In either case, the defendant board will be called upon to give some justification for impinging on the First Amendment interests involved. But, as would be expected, the results differ markedly depending upon the test utilized. Courts that apply a more sympathetic First Amendment view in schoolbook censorship cases generally start with the proposition that limitations on the exercise of these constitutional rights are justified only by the conclusion that the interests of discipline or sound education are materially and substantially jeopardized. This standard derives largely from the case of *Tinker* v. *Des Moines Independent Community School District*,[11] where the Supreme Court held that a junior high school's suspension of three students for wearing black armbands to school to protest the Vietnam war was unconstitutional, as such prohibition of expression of opinion did not materially interfere with the upkeep of appropriate discipline in the operation of the school. This, of course, is a very difficult burden for defendants to meet. For example, in *Minarcini* v. *Strongsville*

City School District,[12] involving the removal of two Kurt Vonnegut books—and, somehow appropriately, Heller's Catch-22—and the replacement of them with the biographies of Captain Eddie Rickenbacker and Herbert Hoover and the Reminiscences of Douglas MacArthur, the Sixth Circuit stated that "the removal of books from a school library is a much more serious burden upon freedom of classroom discussion than the action found unconstitutional in Tinker." In the Massachusetts case, where the defendants—apparently acknowledging that they would be unable to show a substantial government interest in cutting off students' access to the anthology which included a high school girl's poem vividly describing the city as "one million horney lip-smacking men screaming" for specified parts "of my body"—premised their case instead on the assumption that language offensive to the committee and to some parents had no place in the educational system, they were met with the judicial retort that "with the greatest respect to such parents, their sensibilities are not the full measure of what is proper education." But this is hardly the approach of Pico or of Zykan. And if I may venture a guess, it is unlikely to be accepted by the Supreme Court—particularly as it may be augmented in the 1980s.

Because of the difficulty in justifying book removal, the key to succeeding in such a suit is the ability to state a prima facie case of a First Amendment violation. In particular, in such as those of the Second Circuit, where suppression of ideas must be shown, it is crucial to show that students have been limited not only in receiving certain social or political views, but, if possible, that their abilities to express such ideas have been suppressed. In any court, the more the removal of books can be tied to social or political content, the greater the receptivity of the judiciary—a judiciary which, I must stress, is likely to be generally unreceptive to delving into issues of local school administration—to view the state action as constitutionally impermissible. To the degree that the removal of certain books can be characterized as an attempt by the board to block reception by students of certain ideas or ideologies, or even worse, to be viewed as suggesting a disapproval of expression of certain ideas or ideologies, a plaintiff's case is vastly enhanced.

As noted, some courts have held that the personal taste of the board members is insufficient justification for removal of books. Others, such as the Pico court, have required a political purpose—that the exclusion of particular views is motivated by the authorities' opinion about the proper way to organize and run society in general, and that other views will be disapproved; hence, the impermissible suppression. This sort of signaling that certain views are disapproved—resulting in a suppression of ideas— is an important factor in distinguishing and in making susceptible to a lawsuit a book removal situation rather than simply a failure to select a certain book. Removal is a far more understandable form of censorship to the judiciary than is failure to purchase a particular book. It is the targeting by school administrators of particular materials and (at least arguably) the signaling that particular ideas will incur their wrath. As Judge Newman wrote, "The chilling effect of this message on those who would express the idea is all too apparent."

Cases which have the unenviable cast of being labeled as "book tenure cases" (how effectively we damn with slogans!) should not be thought of as standing for the proposition that a book on the shelf actually has tenure. Rather, they should be read as understanding that the suppression of ideas is the natural result of censorship, and that the result is far more emphatically suspect than the far milder impact of not selecting a certain book among many others in a process which necessarily includes as restraining factors the constraints of budget and shelf space, and is based on decisions of relative usefulness.

If possible, of course, counsel representing a plaintiff in such an action could attempt to show, as Judge Newman in his *Pico* concurrence stated, "official conduct that tends to suppress ideas—conduct conveying the message that some idea or viewpoint is not merely unsound, but is not acceptable to be aired within the school community." When clearly defined and carefully planned action to condemn an idea is taken, as the court in *Pico* found it to be, the lawyer's case is made easier. Likewise, a *prima facie* case is more easily established when the books in question contain content clearly of one particular ideology or political view.

The most obvious example of this situation is in the *Nashua* (New Hampshire) case where *Ms.* magazine was banned though *Redbook* and *Mademoiselle* were not. The banning was found to be due to the political content of the magazine, its feminist ideology, rather than the including of articles and advertisements about certain sexual apparati and contraceptives. (In fact, though the defendants' objection to the periodical focused largely on the fact that it contained an advertisement for vibrators, they were particularly unpersuasive in that plaintiff testified that not only did she find *Ms.* of value in her assigned high school courses because of its particular viewpoint, but that she worked afternoons in a store where vibrators were sold.) Likewise, the removal of Vonnegut books and *Catch-22* and their subsequent replacement by books about Eddie Rickenbacker, Hoover, and MacArthur display an obvious political bias. The contrast in those works would go far to convince any court that certain views were not acceptable to the authorities and were sought to be suppressed.

In this vein, it is very important to avoid the type of stipulation which was agreed to by the attorneys in a recent Tenth Circuit case[13] where ten books out of 1,285 were not approved for use in language arts classes in a Colorado school district. Though the banned volumes were such contemporary works as *A Clockwork Orange* and *The Exorcist*, poems by Allan Ginsberg and Ferlinghetti and the like, the parties stipulated that no systematic effort was made "to exclude any particular type of thinking or book." That admission, similar to that of plaintiffs in their brief in *Bicknell*, where it was fairly clearly conceded that there may have been no restriction on freedom of thought or expression, was fatal to plaintiffs' case. Counsel should never enter into such stipulations. I repeat: never.

More difficult are books which do not have clearly oriented political or social views. Generally, works that are held more easily removable are those in which vulgar words or explicit sexual scenes are depicted. If at all possible, I suggest that an attempt should be made to show that such works are reflective of a certain political or social viewpoint, and that the censorship of such works clearly displays to the students a not-so-subtle directive as to what views are unacceptable. A pall of orthodoxy orchestrated by the school board may thus be shown.

What of the hardest case—that involving purportedly vulgar or tasteless passages in a book which is said not to contain a political theme? One answer is to argue that such a book, even if fiction, has a political theme. For example, the poem by the high school girl, illustrating the painful realities of sex in the city with its debasement of a woman's humanity, has a feminist ideology and, especially if neutral books with similar words remain in the library, the ouster could be argued to stem from a kind of political motivation. Likewise, the writings of black authors, even if fiction, often are targeted because they are allegedly in bad taste, contain vulgar epithets, and so forth. Again, it might well be argued that these books are being banned not because of the words and passages contained therein, but because of the school board's aversion to the attitudes and ideologies expressed in the books, or even the racial views of its authors. Of course, the archetypical case on this score was the Mississippi textbook case in which a textbook giving some play to the role and plight of blacks in Mississippi was rejected while a more traditional text was approved.[14]

If it is impossible to categorize the removal of books in such a manner, another tact is available. It might be argued that the words and passages in issue are themselves symbolic and representative of a certain rebellious ideology and that censorship of such works indicates disapproval of what is at its core, a *political* statement made by use of an untraditional means of communication. Certainly George Carlin's radio talk at issue in *Pacifica*[15] is an example of a passage where vulgar words were used to convey a certain—albeit, perhaps, somewhat ambiguous—social and, I believe, political statement. The banning of books with such passages might be argued to lead to the suppression of a more open and less hypocritical social ideology or, at the least, of the views of those who believe that only by speaking freely will people act freely—or differently. This approach is plainly broader than that which would now be approved by most courts. But it is, I suggest, worth the risk of making. Indeed, only if such arguments are made—even to be lost—will it remain possible to continue a broad-based battle against censorship.

A First Amendment Perspective

Floyd Abrams

I particularly want to comment on Professor Yudof's paper. First, the law is and will be, regardless of our preferences, that states are going to make curricular decisions—book publishing, book purchasing, and book removal decisions in most situations will be unencumbered by much court activity. I also have problems and have had, for many years, with the phrase that I consider a rather mischievous one—although I use it on occasion when I have nothing else to say to persuade a judge—which is the public's "right to know." It's very hard to narrow it from a strictly analytic point of view. And it's very hard to explain why the public has a right to know this and not that. So I fully agree with Professor Yudof about that. And I agree as well that some kind of due process notions sometimes help. Whether it is an irrevocable delegation theory or a procedural due process theory, sometimes the school boards don't follow their own regulations and so there are some advantages to be had from that.

I do not agree that the definitional difficulties which Professor Yudof reports ought to deter us, at least as litigators, from prosecuting and from pursuing certain themes in the cases. The difficulty of defining academic freedom, for example, is not something that will stop an awful lot of courts. And the difficulty of advising the court on orthodoxy is a problem, but it is a litigation problem. There must be some set of facts by which the party prosecuting a case like this just can't lose. It is intolerable from a societal point of view to have school boards throw out the liberal books every four years and throw out the conservative books every four years. And that, I tell you instinctively, the courts will buy. We have to figure out how to phrase it, but I think that they will not allow this society to become one in which school boards have elections based on political ideology.

Any kind of First Amendment due process argument is a watered-down First Amendment argument. In general, it is just saying people have to do things in the right way, have to follow the right procedures or constitutional procedures. And from a tricky litigation point of view, it's an argument worth making again because the school boards in some of these cases act in such a bizarre fashion that I think that you can make something of it. I don't really think though, on a long-range basis, that that's going to persuade the big courts, but so far so good.

It seems to me that there was more diffidence and more indecisiveness in that part of Dr. O'Neil's paper which dealt with whether objections ought to be made to people ("censors") on the Left, or the more "progressive" side, or to the "good guys"—women, minorities, other groups. That is a very dangerous doctrine. You will lose any sense of First Amendment legitimacy if this comes to be viewed as a liberal against conservative thing, as opposed to a First Amendment thing which goes in all ways. This should not degenerate into a political contest as opposed to a principled First Amendment one.

I come to you with ten commandments, ten points, and they're all brief.

TEN COMMANDMENTS FOR LITIGATION

First, bring good cases. That's a very hard one. But there are so many cases already in the literature, where the school boards have acted in a goofy manner, a manner against which almost any intelligent person will rebel, even if he has to overcome it because of legal doctrine which tells him that the courts can't get involved with what they think are school board decisions. But it really is important to pick the right cases. That's a major reason for holding this conference.

Second, you've got to recognize that it's going to be very hard to create any doctrine of law which is going to win many cases in this area. Not because it's new, but because it asks so much of the courts; it risks so much in the way of judicial involvement, in areas in which they instinctively believe that they ought not to be involved. Notwithstanding the Sixth Circuit opinion,[1] the Massachusetts opinion,[2] and a flock of other victories obtained in this area, you really have to start your analysis by saying that it's going to be difficult to create any winning, long-range strategy on a continuing basis. All the more reason, if you can, to pick the best cases, the most absurd cases, the most frightening cases, the most politicized cases, if you can do it—and to try to get the courts into the area, court by court, until they can't get out anymore.

Third, this is a useful area to have detailed pleadings—to really smoke out your opponent, in a situation in which you're very likely to be met with a motion to dismiss, if not one for summary judgment. Say what you have to say in the complaint itself, so it will not then be a lawyer's argument after the fact, justifying the complaint, but something which is in the complaint itself and harder for a judge to overlook. At least a situation will develop where, applying normal legal instincts, the court will be hard put to just throw you out because it thinks that you shouldn't be bringing this kind of case in the first place.

Next, discover, discover, and discover. Discovery is terrific in these areas. Very often, people who do these things are idiots. They're fools. They cannot justify what they do. They can't speak an English sentence. They don't know the books they've banned. They don't know the rules they have violated. These are marvelous things to get in front of the court, in the motion practice stage, and, of course, in terms of winning the case.

I don't see enough use of expert testimony in terms of the legal theories, to make them work. If you have to show a pall of orthodoxy, why can't you come up with a social scientist—surely you can—who will say that there will be a pall of orthodoxy if this book or that book is out. And you can do some polls. There are things which social scientists can do which will be helpful and have the effect of beating down any motion directed at your complaint. At least you will have some kind of triable issue of fact. That's obviously one of the first things you want.

Next, you really have to use all areas of constitutional law that come to mind, including due process and First Amendment theories. I don't agree, however, with a general buckshot method of throwing twenty-five different theories at the court. The courts just won't take any of them seriously. But if you do pick a few theories, whatever will work there, you ought not to be limited to a substantive First Amendment analysis.

It is necessary for you to be very bold, from a theoretical First Amendment point of view. This is a very difficult area instinctively to get the courts into. And if that is true, you ought to take more risks than you might otherwise to get the courts to buy a First Amendment theory that does not come easy to them—even if they say that they are taking the book out of the library because the words are unfit for children, and even if there's no sign of a strictly political motivation. Arguments remain available that almost any kind of withdrawal from the body politic, or the body social, of language like this, is a political act. I mean that not as rhetoric; I mean it as something which I think one could argue.

My ninth point is don't be political. This is not a political struggle— if you mean it to be a First Amendment matter—against conservatives, even though conservatives may be against you very often. It just won't work to get up in court and be perceived as taking what some judges would think of as the liberal orthodox point of view against the Right and not doing it against the Left.

Finally, stay out of the Supreme Court. You really don't want to go there yet. If you can, create a body of law around the country, with different courts putting their foot into this water, step by step, dealing with a number of bad cases arising where you can build some body of law, and then someday you may have to go to the Supreme Court. But it would be better if *they* took you to the Supreme Court, rather than you taking them. It would be better, of course, to win some case in a court of appeals and have the other side take you up. It's not a good time for cases like this in the Supreme Court. In a lot of these cases, you wouldn't get any votes in the Supreme Court at all, not even the liberal votes. It's a very hard area. So build up a body of district court and, where necessary, court of appeals or state appellate court, case law. Take some losses, if you have to, and only go the superappellate route if you have a terrific set of facts, or if you're simply impelled by the exigencies of a particular case. I really don't think that the Sixth Circuit opinion[3] would get a single vote on this court. You have to limit your expectations of what you can do, short term, in the area. Win as many as you can, in different places. When the day comes that either you go to the court or someone takes you to the court, there'll be fifteen, twenty-five, cases—notwithstanding the obvious lack of doctrinal consistency among them—where at least courts will have gotten into it. It can then be argued, "Look, it worked out all right. The courts got in just that much, no more; just that book, just that ruling; a specific injunction; you can do this narrowly, all these things are possible."

Let me try to leave you with a note of cheer. This is a very interesting area. I do appreciate that there is no way that you can create the world that a litigating lawyer would want for you—absurd school boards violating their own regulations for purely political purposes, plainly recorded on leaflets they've handed out—then it's wonderful. But if you do get a case like that (and *Pico* was pretty close to that), that's the kind of case to go with. A final, institutional note. Stay in consultation with each other, with organizations that are active in this area, with the entities which are knowledgeable in the area, to share some ideas and not plunge headlong into what may be the creation of a very bad—from your point of view— body of case law.

THIRD GENERAL SESSION

Current and Future Litigation, a Panel Discussion

Panelists: Charles Halpern and Joel Klein

Mr. Halpern:

My real task is to share some observations about litigation strategies based on my experience as a public interest lawyer. Since 1966 I have given thought at various times to how you create a body of law. How do you get lawyers involved? How do you draw together client and constituent groups from selective service law, mental health law, environmental law, consumer law, communications law, and other areas?

There were a few premises that were never really articulated by Floyd Abrams with which I have some real problems. First, there was his insistence that we are dealing with an apolitical problem that should be addressed in an apolitical fashion. At various times, it's important that we present ourselves as apolitical. But we are dealing with what is, at its core, a political problem, and we should integrate our litigation strategies into a larger political strategy.

Floyd Abrams' second premise was the assumption that in planning litigation we have infinite resources. The dirty little secret, for lawyers generally, is money. And if we are partners at Cahill, Gordon and we do our litigation for the *New York Times*, the habit of not thinking about money problems is adaptive to our professional lives. For those of us who are public interest lawyers, it is not very adaptive. The cost of depositions goes up weekly or monthly. Furthermore, the idea that resources are infinite also leads one away from the most important issue in litigation strategy and that is case selection. If you have infinite resources, you just challenge censorship wherever it raises its ugly head. If you do not have infinite resources, you have to think more tactically in the cases you take on.

That leads to my third problem with Floyd Adams' presentation. There was an underlying lawyer's assumption that you measure your success or failure by winning cases. It is possible to win cases that leave you farther behind than if you had lost. It is possible to get a verdict in favor of your client that is still a defeat. And it's possible to win some cases, or a whole series of cases, that may still not address the real problem that you're concerned with. For example, the suggestion that the focus of litigation efforts should be on "goofy" school boards is a great mistake. We're dealing with threats to our liberties that have little to do with goofy school boards. It's great fun for lawyers to deal with goofy school boards and to depose the redneck yahoos and expose them for the prejudiced fools they are. But if we are dealing with a national, well-coordinated, richly financed, and highly sophisticated movement, challenging goofy school boards strikes me as perhaps taking our attention away from the areas where it ought to be focused.

The first premise, as I've just suggested, is that we are entering a period of repression in which the pall of orthodoxy may well be no exaggeration. I'm a little embarrassed, frankly, when I talk about the pall of orthodoxy that flows from the censorship of school libraries. But if you see that phenomenon in a larger context of well-orchestrated, well-financed, systematic efforts to impose certain orthodox views on a society, then I don't think it is embarrassing. That is the kind of challenge that we ought to address. That challenge will have to be dealt with in political terms. That does not mean that litigation is irrelevant, not at all. But it does mean that litigation efforts should be thought of in the broader political context and that an eye to political alliances must always be kept—when choosing cases, choosing how to publicize them, choosing how to use them to build constituencies. It is not sufficient to simply energize First Amendment devotees. Most of us here are people with special enthusiasm for different parts of the Constitution. And so long as it's just we First Amendment folks who are engaged in this political battle, we lose.

My next premise is that there are very few warriors and very little money to wage this battle. Alan Levine tells me that the *Pico* case has cost more than $50,000. That's a lot of money; we're not going to fight many *Pico* cases, I guess. Happily, in our coalition it looks like there are some deep pockets. We're going to have to think about how we use our resources and how we use the lawyers and other people who have advocacy skills for these struggles. And we're going to have to use them carefully and well.

The next premise deals with selection. The goofy school

board case, which may be the most winnable case in the short run, may not be the case in which we want to sink our limited resources of money and manpower. It seems to me that another criterion for case selection is the extent to which a particular instance of school book censorship is a manifestation of the national effort to repress ideas which are unacceptable to those organizations which are promoting censorship—to show that this is not a localized decision by the local school board but part of a national strategy. Another way of selecting cases that will help to deal with the motivational problem is to show that the attack on a few particular school books is not an isolated effort by these kooks on the school board; but it is really part of a coordinated effort in a particular region, to rid it of a whole range of things which are unpopular and unacceptable to the anxious would-be censors. Here is another way of showing this as a piece of a larger strategy. If a defense fund is established, and you're given three cases—one, kook school boards; two, a manifestation of national strategy; three, part of a local strategy of cleansing an area of the unclean—and you have limited funds to allocate, my suggestion is that those funds go to the second and third types of cases. You've got to be asking how this litigation fits into what we see as a very broad-based and systematic effort to ring down a pall of orthodoxy.

A final premise, that again grows out of varied experience, is that coordination among lawyers and interested groups is critical. They have to have information about what the others are doing; they have to have information about what has worked and what has not worked—and I don't mean just cases, but also other effective ways of resisting censorship efforts.

One important concept in thinking about litigation strategy and assessing prospects for success comes from a law teacher named Mark Galanter. It is the idea of "repeat players" and "one-shot players." His theory is that repeat players are, because of the architecture of the American justice system, systematically more likely to prevail; and one-shot players are systematically more likely to lose. That has very much reflected my experience of the legal system, both as a public interest lawyer and a corporate lawyer. Corporate lawyers are classically repeat players; the corporations are always doing business in the same form, with the same problems, and they shape the law to meet their interests. What has been distinctive about public interest law since the NAACP Legal Defense Fund pioneered the process in the 1930s is the idea that public interest lawyers and their clients try to be repeat players, try to think about not just a single individual case, but a case as it fits into a long-term strategy. The early desegregation cases showed this very systematically. When the NAACP was picking out cases, they brought cases that were easy at first, or at least relatively easy. They built on their earlier cases. They had some sense of bringing the country along through public education. At a certain point, they started to integrate legislative strategies with their litigation strategies. They played like classic repeat players. And that is one of the lessons we have learned that should not be lost in this effort.

One of the problems that we've had in learning this lesson is that everything that we do educates the opposition. Some of you may have heard about the emergence in the last couple of years of a really quite enormous development of so-called right-wing public interest law firms. They're funded by corporations. They pursue conservative causes. They have learned these lessons. The goofy school boards are the classic one-shot players. We will not have the luxury of dealing with those people very much longer. Those people and their lawyers are soon going to be as sophisticated as we are. My guess is—and this is pure speculation—that this is not the only meeting of this kind going on. Those folks are holding similar meetings; if they're not, they're going to very shortly. The techniques that I'm talking about are not news to them. James Watt, the current Secretary of the Interior, is a product of the right-wing public interest law firms. He has for the last several years been doing antienvironmental litigation in the Rocky Mountains. Whether that group is also into schoolbook censorship, I don't know. But they are part of a nationwide network of right-wing firms; they have excellent communications; they do not have cash bars when they meet, believe me.

I've said something about political coalition building. The First Amendment constituency isn't enough. If we see schoolbook censorship as a larger part of an effort to impose certain lifestyles in society, that might give us an idea around which very much larger constituencies can be organized to oppose censorship, if you can make sufficient connections. There are the obvious groups, women's groups and the like, but also the enormous, not very well-organized groups in the society that are committed to alternative lifestyles. Now, I don't believe that the Moral Majority is a majority anymore. If you put together all the people who are committed to the living-on-the-earth lifestyle, the sexual-experimentation lifestyle, the recreational-use-of-drugs lifestyle, and the variety of other kinds of experiments that are abroad in the land today, you have a larger constituency. Will the people who have those kinds of commitments feel threatened enough so that they can be activated in some way?

In thinking about litigation in context, you consider the kinds of cases you want to devote limited resources to. Lawyers are not always, and perhaps not even usually, the best people to make these kinds of judgments. Lawyers are going to be oriented toward winning cases. That will systematically bias them in the direction of winnable cases. Other people might have different agendas, might like to take more of a risk, or see significant benefits from taking an important case, giving it the best shot they can, and losing it. Lots of progress has come about through losing cases. Considerations of likelihood of success, on the other hand, are things which lawyers can probably advise on, and that is one criterion to consider. Whether it's premature to bring a case, whether it jumps some steps in the development, and the like, are questions that ought to be asked. Certainly there is a great tradition of starting with the easiest cases and moving on to the harder cases. Now, I'm oversimplifying, because no litigators ever have that much coordination or that much control over what goes on around the country. But there are ways in which centralized bodies like this group in conference can encourage or discourage certain kinds of litigation. We are here talking about extremely difficult cases. School libraries strike me as an incredibly difficult problem. It is very much harder, for example, than taking books off the shelves in a general library. Before we go all out and say we should get these issues before the courts, let's ask whether we really want to focus on the *school* library, as we're asking the courts to do. We're going to be pulled into these cases somehow; nobody is going to control this altogether. But there is a role for coordination and leadership. And, to my way of thinking, people should be discouraged from taking on very hard cases, particularly since there can be a real down side to this litigation. You can make bad law, you can win cases on grounds which are going to lead to results and consequences that you don't like. Another thing about seeing litigation in context is to make sure that you don't oversell the potential of litigation. It's expensive and slow and it's a blunt, crude instrument. It also can exact a tremendous personal toll on the people who put themselves forward as litigants. Not to undersell litigation either, but again, it's terribly important to see the variety of other alternatives.

Again, in terms of thinking strategically, there are two kinds of candidates for the best cases. One is the case in which you can show an integrated national effort to impose values. The other is the one in which you can show an integrated *local* effort to deal not only with school textbooks, but also with television content, with the kinds of public forums that are available, how gays are treated under municipal law, a whole cluster of issues which are likely to emerge together.

A final thought on litigation that comes out of Floyd Abrams' comment is to avoid the Supreme Court. This has been kind of horn-book doctrine for us for almost ten years now. The days when people said, "Let's get this one resolved by the Supreme Court," are long behind us. Note, however, that if you win a case in the court of appeals, it's very hard for you to keep that case out of the Supreme Court. You know, the people who lost have the right to seek *certiorari*, and while you can oppose it, the matter is pretty much out of your hands at that point. It's a caution, that's all.

A few prescriptions grow out of this. The first, obviously, is to keep an eye on the big picture. The second is to gather as much information as is possible and disseminate it to interested lawyers and interested nonlawyers who are concerned with these matters. The possibility of inventing some kind of reporter service may be a good one, although it may well be that the ALA *Newsletter on Intellectual Freedom* takes care of that need already. Every law library in the country, certainly every law school, should be getting it. And, of course, the public education issues also deserve continuing attention. Somebody, in some kind of ongoing way, should be looking at the cases as they emerge, developing a long-term strategy, and deciding which cases fit best. There are some cases where it might be worth doing really extensive discovery, even hundreds of thousands of dollars of discovery to reveal the network of forces that are brought into focus in a particular censorship case. The kind of public education effects of that kind of discovery effort would be tremendous. It may well be worth putting $100,000 into that one case, rather than $5,000 dollars into twenty cases. Finally, some thought must be directed to the situation of the people who are out on the battle lines right now. How do you provide for support and encouragement for the librarians, the school teachers, and others who are out there waging the day-to-day, low visibility struggle against censorship efforts? Litigation backup might not be available to each of them in each of their travails. That is holding out a false promise and it is, to my way of thinking, also a strategy which in the long-term is counterproductive. The dilemma of supporting and encouraging those people is one in which nonlegal strategy should be emphasized.

POLITICAL STRATEGIES

Mr. Klein:

Relevant to your proceedings, I've spent the last three years as part of the J. P. Stevens Amalgamated Clothing Workers' fight as an attorney for the clothing workers. The utilization of litigation there as part of an overall political strategy and its dovetailing is a very important model. It's a model that I think the public interest bar has not assessed as well as it could. It was Arthur Goldberg, general counsel of the clothing workers in New York, who took one of the most remarkable pieces of political strategy and put it together, including some very interesting litigation strategy. You would benefit to go outside of the public interest bar into a bit more of the "blood and guts" kind of economic fighting that goes on in the labor management area.

My basic thesis is that Charlie Halpern is right: winning is not what you're about. What you're about is insuring that you continue to play in the courts. So long as you continue to play, so long as the doors stay open, the effect can only be good. It is a political problem. Among the political systems in America that are going to be most sympathetic to the view of the First Amendment crew here assembled are the courts. That is the best shot you have. The Supreme Court of the United States today, awful though it might be in many people's eyes, is a far better forum in which to have these issues resolved than most other nonjudicial forums. To the extent that you keep that body open, ultimately it's in your interest. The problem is to prevent your own political, moral zeal from taking you so far out that you have doors closed to you. There are areas where that kind of development has happened.

I am troubled by the fact that you are a litigation-oriented body, by and large without a constituency. And that has its problems. Lawyers like the courtroom. One of the reasons you're less effective is because you like to resolve cases in courtrooms. One of the things you can learn from the Amalgamated Clothing Workers is that all the lawyers in the world are useless if you don't have the right organizers. Effectiveness comes from using the lawyer truly as the hired gun, not in the pejorative sense, but in the sense that somebody else has a game plan to be implemented, and knows what role we have to play. One of the problems in this kind of organization, and to some extent in the public interest bar, is that lawyers are their own constituency. That hurts them in many ways. In that sense, they're not getting across to courts either, who often have different views than the First Amendment view here. You're missing the input from people whom you have to hear, the people who will ultimately be affected by the rulings. And that's an uncomfortable process.

I, for example, represent the parents of many mentally retarded people involved in litigation over deinstitutionalization. That is a very hard group to represent, yet dealing with them has increased my courtroom efficacy. One, it's a real group. They have no particular interest in what my views on deinstitutionalization are. They know what their views are. Their children and their loved ones are affected. The court feels it's got a real player. Most judges in America feel equally capable of making value judgments. To the extent that a court perceives that what this litigation is about is that you, the ACLU, or the right-to-read group, or whatever, thinks children ought to read more Eldridge Cleaver and less something else—the less effective you are.

It is different if you have a constituency. Parents are an important constituency for you, and that's going to take some education. Many parents' groups are not going to be sympathetic at first. But I think most parents don't want their children's access quite so limited as perhaps some of the new waves in America would like. So there's a constituency to develop.

In addition, I would shamelessly develop the publishing constituency and study the economics of it. It is foolhardy for public interest lawyers who are going to do First Amendment work on book access not to understand the economics of publishing. If this movement is simply a values movement, then the publishing industry, because of its sympathetic views on the First Amendment, will help you out. But they're not going to be a particular ally. If this movement has significant implications for the economics of the major publishing industries, then you will get all the economic help you need. Somehow that makes people uncomfortable, as if the First Amendment were up for sale in any shape or form, but that betrays a political naivete. Because if it is a political fight, what you want are your economic allies. They will stay the duration.

As to the goofy school board point that was raised earlier—having done the Stevens campaign, and J. P. Stevens was represented by some pretty well-heeled lawyers with a *lot* of southern, conservative, quasi-public-interest organizations on the other side, the right-to-work groups and whatever not wanting the economic wherewithal—when you got down to the first level, to the plant level, even with all the lawyers in the world, people betrayed their real selves. The people on the front line *will* betray their religious zeal. That's exactly what happened in the J. P. Stevens affair. They lost the sense of balance that would have enabled them to be effective and simply had this real moral righteousness. The lesson to be learned is that to the extent that we indulge that moral righteousness, we undermine our own efficacy. So you *can* go after the so-called goofy school board, *not* to show it as aberrant— quite the contrary—but to show it as really quite typical.

The case that I would use is not the odd book. While I agree with the principle, I would avoid the dirty book because it's not the most powerful case. Nor would I particularly look for the one book that might be the controversial book that most of us think is critical and should be in the libraries. Rather, look for the pattern and process. Try to show in the courtroom how this particular school district decides to put together a curriculum. Try to discover that process and show the court, so to say, that this is *not* a way to run a railroad, that this process is subject to inherent abuse. In that sense, your winning of cases becomes quite important. Because what the court is trying to do is assure, at least nationwide, that the grosser abuses are remedied. If the judge shares your political philosophy and is willing to go with it, you don't have to worry. You don't need this meeting. I've tried cases before judges who were way ahead of me, and I want to come back to the point about keeping cases out of the Supreme Court. Keeping judges who are way ahead of you in line is also a skill worth learning, in terms of playing again the next day. The challenge is the guy who's different. I clerked for Justice Powell on the United States Supreme Court. Justice Powell didn't grow up on the streets of New York City. He doesn't share my sense of guerrilla warfare in everything in life. To go into his courtroom and convince him that Little Italy is where the action is, is preposterous. There are more Justice Powells in this country's courts than Joel Kleins. That will continue to be the norm. On the other hand, he's a person who will listen and I think if he's persuaded that our concern is the real potential for abuse, for curtailing knowledge, for limiting learning, by any yahoo group on the Left or on the Right, that judge will do something in these cases for you.

LEGAL STRATEGIES

There has been a lot of discussion on theory. It's a combination of the access problem with the inevitable one-only selection—you can't have fourteen history textbooks in a class. Those are somewhat difficult conceptual problems. I wouldn't spend a lot of time on theoretical issues if I were going to be litigating a case. These are fact cases, and if you win these cases, you win them on facts. That's why discovery is critical. It may be that the economics of discovery are painful, but if you don't do it, you're left with rhetoric. If you don't *show* the abuses in the process, then you're just up there with pious incantations. If you can show in court that the Moral Majority's got this well-heeled effort and that costs you a quarter of a million dollars, that's the best quarter of a million dollars you'll spend. If you *can't* show it, but claim it and yell about it, then you've hurt your cause immeasurably. Likewise, I disagree with Charlie Halpern that you ought to tie censorship into lifestyle and homosexuality issues and counterculture issues. That's far, far down the line. There's nothing worse than going into a case that involves book removal and saying what's at stake here is diversity and lifestyle. That lacks an initial credibility. Over a five-year litigation, you may convert any jurist. But to begin with, your credibility is very important.

It is better to focus on the facts, put them in the complaint. Don't be afraid of the case. If you've got a shot at a winner, tell the court what it is. Don't try to give it twenty-three different theories of the First Amendment or of the facts. Pick the best one you've got, or the best two, and take your shot. Brainstorm a lot in those late-night sessions before you go into court. That's what's important about a case like the *Pico* case in the Second Circuit. They put in time and found their theories. They may not win in the end. History may reflect they *didn't* have the best theory. But they went in there and worked it through. That smorgasbord effect doesn't work. Most lawyers are so afraid that they don't have "the" answer that they throw in fourteen different counts, diffusing the effect.

Courts know what's going on. There's enough play in the joints of the First Amendment doctrine to begin to write, if not a coherent ideological or neutral-principles result, at least an opinion that's *plausible*. Lawyers are terribly afraid of motivational analysis, but it gives you, again, play in the joints in difficult cases. A district court making findings of fact on motivation will make the right findings if the district court is upset with what's going on. The Supreme Court can't review them all. Even the courts of appeals aren't going to review all the fact-findings. So a motivational test, while perhaps not appealing to the purist in most of us and while perhaps presenting litigation problems, will give the district court some play, too.

I do think you're going to have a relatively easy time on the library removal type of cases. I was present at a Supreme Court argument in the *Jacobs* v. *School Board of Indiana* case in 1974,[1] involving dirty words in school newspapers. The school board's lawyer got up—and this is a classic issue where zeal, moral passion, and a sense of virtue can kill an argument—and said to the court, "You know, our school board is totally consistent on it. It's not as if we say the kids can't write it in the school newspaper and then we allow *Lady Chatterly's Lover* in the library." She said, "No, in our school board we've cleansed the library, we've cleansed the magazines." Justice Stewart looked down—and he was marvelous on this—and said, "Well, this is a much harder case if we have your libraries up here, isn't it?" That's the kind of reaction you're going to get. If *Pico* goes to the Supreme Court, I think it will fare quite well up there. The court is going to be bothered by that kind of approach. They're not going to take the approach that in the school library anything goes. But people on the United States Supreme Court are troubled, even in a school library context, about taking books off shelves.

The harder thing is the selection policy; that is the issue of trying to decide which textbooks go where. That is going to be a process issue for you. You may win it using the sort of theory that Professor Yudof expressed. At best, you're going to get the courts to say, "God, this is an awful way that they're doing it. We've got to do something." That's a "shocks-the-conscience" kind of case. If indeed you get offensively racist literature forced on children in schools, some court will figure out, assisted by some clever law professor, how to write an opinion to get the job done.

Set up your litigation by going for real plaintiffs. Avoid plaintiffs who let you control the litigation. Try to get parents' groups, publishing companies, and the like. What bothers a lot of appellate courts, and particularly today's United States Supreme Court, is lawyer's litigation. I recently argued one, representing the parents' group for institutionalized people, in the Supreme Court; and one of the few questions asked of me, and it was on rebuttal by Justice Blackmun, was, "Do all the parents belong to this group?" That was something that concerned him. The issue is having a real constituency. The United States Supreme Court, whatever else it is, is not an unsophisticated body—and if the Justices think you're simply taking a political fight and trying to dress it up in a legal complaint, they're going to respond against that. If they think you're carrying a client's fight, they're going to respond better to it, though it might not get you home. So work through the plaintiff's issue and keep them involved in the litigation. Get their involvement on the record. Make the affirmative side of your case. Courts will respond better to the real concerns of Charlie Halpern, parent, than to some of the political concerns of Charlie Halpern, public interest lawyer. Get the real concerns on the record.

Pleadings, my dear friends of the ACLU, are about nouns and verbs and not about adjectives and adverbs. If you have the facts, somebody else will say that this is outrageous. Your assurance will do nothing for them. Indeed, it will turn most people precisely the other way. Underwrite your pleadings. Tell people what happened, but don't say, "this abhorrent practice, this outrageous practice." It simply doesn't work. If you start out in a case by trying to throw down the gauntlet, and the other side doesn't pick it up, be assured the judge will. It's in his or her nature.

Should we lose cases on appeal so that we can keep them out of the United States Supreme Court? Well, there is a certain truth to this, and this is where I think those of you who are engaged in a political strategy need to have your client's cooperation. But if your client calls the shots and your client is hell-bent, you've got to be hell-bent. In most of the public interest litigation that I've been recently involved with (like the Mental Health Law Project), you can often get your client to work with you on long-term strategy because clients in this area are not like IBM which has a particular dollar amount due in a case and can't afford not to litigate. Most clients in this case want to be around for another day, too. The notion of modest gains is important. If you've got a district court that's going to write an opinion that's sure to get reversed, it's your job to make that opinion one that's easy to preserve, to help the judge leave behind some of his or her ideological or moral zeal.

The other thing that's perfectly plausible is to settle cases. If you win a big case in the court of appeals but think it's the kind of case in which the United States Supreme Court is going to clean house on you, I think you should settle. A

case which should have been settled like that and wasn't was
the case of *Bartley v. Kremens.*[2] Another case involved hospi-
talization of juveniles in the mental health area. The lower
courts uniformly do well by these issues. Not good things in
terms of the American Psychiatric Association but in terms
of due process models, keeping children out of hospitals. You
don't have to apply it to four-year-olds, or seven-year-olds.
You don't have to have a precommitment hearing; you can
have a hearing within forty-eight hours. You don't have so
many lawyers in the process. Once you proceed with the
whole thing, you may lose the entire thing, which is what
happened in the Supreme Court. The Chief Justice got a
chance to write a large counterideological response.

Don't be afraid to cut back your winnings. The worst
that could ensue would be a decision that the choice of library
or classroom textbooks is somehow nonjusticiable, or somehow it's inherently within the discretion of the school. One
opinion of that sort means that next month we'll have to find
another First Amendment issue with which to concern ourselves. So stay away from that. If you continue to keep the fires
going, the courts will ultimately be your allies. There'll be a
lot of small victories in the townships of America—that is, on
the individual school board level. It may mean less glory in the
headlines but more books in the library.

AMICUS CURIAE EFFORTS

R. Bruce Rich:

I'd like the panel's views on the efficacy of *amicus curiae* efforts
within the broader litigation strategy.

Mr. Klein:

I have represented the APA as *amicus.* My strategy on *amicus
curiae* is probably different from many. Proliferation of *amici*
briefs is the greatest mistake that ever came down the pike.
In a case where ten organizations file briefs, most of them are
not going to be read. If only we could somehow figure out a
way to eliminate the egos involved! What you've got to do is
get those ten groups to sign on to one well-written brief. That
brief has to add to the plaintiff's brief, or the defendant's brief.
For example, in a recent case, what we tried to do was write
a brief on the developmental disabilities act; then we got a
consortium of groups together and they put together a brief
on the policy. I would not, in most cases, propound an alterna-

tive legal theory. For one thing, you've got to figure out which legal theory is going to fly and give it your best shot. If you support more than one position, you begin to get a smorgasbord effect, especially in appellate courts, and particularly in the United States Supreme Court. There are nine people up there. If you fractionate, you undercut your credibility and hurt your case. The best reason to file an *amicus* brief is because you think your side of the case is not being argued very well and you're dissatisfied with the lawyer. The other point is that the opportunity for *amicus* presentations in district court shouldn't be overlooked as it often is; it's often very useful.

R. Bruce Rich:

I might add two perspectives from AAP's own experience with *amici curiae*. First, a useful function we've been able to perform in the *amicus* area has not necessarily been to articulate legal theories or even factual concepts that weren't adequately developed in the record, but rather to add a unique or deeper perspective of the potential implications for a given sector—in our case, the publishers. I question to some extent Joel Klein's notion that a single, unitary *amicus* brief would necessarily accomplish that. For example, in *Pico,* while there were a fairly significant number of briefs filed with the court of appeals, taken together they lent a number of useful perspectives—those of different interested communities, although I would have liked to see somewhat greater coordination. I look to Alan Levine's reaction as to whether he felt that served a useful function.

Alan Levine:

There really were different constituents represented by the *amicus* briefs, to say nothing of organizational and personal rivalries. Would more coordination have been possible? Perhaps. We had a few meetings, but they were not terribly productive. I'm not sure they influenced the direction in which any of the briefs went. When I was with the CLU, we got away from writing *amicus* briefs and now that's the policy of the CLU. *Amicus* briefs are the exception. I'm not sure I have any better judgment than anybody else reading the *Pico* opinions as to the impact of *amicus* briefs. But I do share Joel's suspicion that their proliferation probably meant that most, if not all, simply were not read by the court and that if the numbers could be reduced from eight to two, that perhaps would be more productive.

Judith Krug:

I represent a constituency which does a lot of its litigative work through *amicus curiae* briefs. This is a general comment: We are anxious to provide such support. We can't do that unless we know the issues that are being litigated at the various levels. It is incumbent on the counsel to develop his issues and list them so that we can follow them, develop our briefs, and file on time. By and large, I'm attempting to give my counsel direction, but often I'm flying in the dark.

Mr. Klein:

Bruce Rich stresses that you should file an *amicus* because there is something there for the court to hear which isn't directly related to the legal issues. You want the court to hear it. If the judge doesn't read it before the argument, it's not worth anything to you. Even if there are eight different perspectives, you've got to narrow them down; at most, one or two or three really mean something to the United States Supreme Court or to the court of appeals. If you don't do that, eight people may feel they've been heard, but you've eliminated the possibility of getting in the one or two things that will affect the decisionmaking process.

Unidentified Speaker:

I have to agree with the assertion you made earlier that one of the major problems in these cases is to build constituencies and to let the court know that there are constituencies out there who care about these cases, who care about this particular case. In fact, that's one of the major functions of the *amicus* brief. And I think it's a mistake to denigrate that importance. I'm not actually sure whether in some cases it may be that that idea is better expressed by ten different briefs than by ten organizations on one brief, but that's a tactical question. I don't think we can ignore the importance of that constituency building and to informing the court that, yes, there are constituencies out there who care about this issue. So, therefore, I think it's a mistake to denigrate the importance of that.

Diane Shugert:

In our organization, the National Council of Teachers of English, we filed an *amicus* brief, a separate one, in the *Pico* case. It was the very first time our organization had ever done such a thing. The money to pay for it was raised by twenty-five and fifty dollar contributions from state organizations who felt strongly about this issue. Other money was raised nationally.

We were the client of the attorneys who filed that brief. We did not enter that case for our own egos, but because the lead attorney and the foundation got involved and felt that they wanted us included. We made an extra effort because it was a necessary kind of thing. Really, most of the nonprofit groups that are functioning in this simply want to support the larger issue. And if not filing an *amicus* brief will support it, we will not file it.

Alan Levine:

Let me go back to the issue of constituencies. Lawyers are inclined to look at narrow legal issues, to aim for courtroom victories, and they aren't very good at the political part of it. From my own experience in NYCLU and looking now at the ACLU, I think this has always been a fundamental problem with the ACLU and perhaps most of the other "cause" organizations represented here. Hardnosed political organizing should be done around these cases so that constituencies, to some limited extent, can be built into cases. I'm sure that Jonathan Shapiro, in putting together the *Chelsea* case[3] and making the lead plaintiff the Right to Read Defense Committee, intended showing the court that there was a constituency, that it wasn't just a couple of individual plaintiffs. The *Presidents Council* case[4] had that terribly awkward name because there was a group called the Presidents Council of all the PTAs in District 25 in Queens which desperately wanted to be represented and show their support of the case. That case, perhaps more than any other that I was ever involved in for the ACLU, continually had the client's interest in mind. To some extent, this places a burden on the lawyers, but it is also very helpful in keeping the issue in the public eye.

How much attention is generally paid by groups to the constituency they represent when they file *amicus* briefs? I suspect that these briefs get written in lawyers' offices and that the constituencies aren't involved. You can rally those people to play a role in a case like *Pico* that's different from an *amicus* brief. But if that case goes back to trial, it will be an enormous and costly undertaking. Discovery will be very important. It has been suggested that massive efforts should be devoted to showing the origins of this particular book banning. We know the origins were a parents' conference; we also know that there was literature from the Heritage Foundation. It would certainly appear to relate to other controversies. But that should be fully fleshed out for the court. If they want us to prove ideological motivation here—I think it exists—

then it's going to be very, very expensive. There's no reason why, if we go back to court and I'm the lawyer and the NYCLU has one of its lawyers on it, that the NCTE shouldn't have one of its lawyers, and the ALA, and any other organization. If there are then funds to feed into the lawsuit, it would be much more productive to feed it into discovery than into an *amicus* brief.

Judith Krug:

That's fine as long as we have a say in the development of those issues. The money comes with strings, and the strings are that we want the issues that concern us considered. Until we get that, the strings are going to be very short.

Kenneth Norwick:

As one who has litigated some First Amendment cases and is also a full-time lobbyist for the NYCLU and, to some extent, the ACLU, I have some comments. Based on our discussions, I sense litigation may be the most pessimistic, the most difficult, the most expensive way of accomplishing our goals. I know this is a litigation conference, but can we achieve some of our goals before going to court by having a hand in developing the process? We've heard that word over and over again—process. If the process that the school board, or the legislature, or the state bureaucracy is developing is a process of library selection or deselection, then the question becomes, Should our constituencies be actively involved in the development of that process even if that means having to compromise? Or do you want to stay outside with your constituencies and then attack? The other question is, To what extent do you keep litigation strategy in mind when you participate in the process?

Burton Joseph:

Ken's book, *Lobbying for Freedom*, St. Martin's Press, is really very good in terms of the political aspect of the First Amendment, as distinguished from the litigation component. Perhaps one of the panel members would like to respond to Ken's observations.

Mr. Klein:

In deciding whether to participate in those kinds of programs, you have to decide how likely you are to achieve what you want through participation. If you think it's an absolute lost cause and your only hope is litigation, you should stay out. Since litigation isn't an all-purpose *nostrum*, many situations will arise in which you'd not want to go into it.

Kenneth Norwick:
>What about drafting a model textbook selection process?

Mr. Klein:
>Absolutely.

Kenneth Norwick:
>Do it?

Mr. Klein:
>Absolutely.

Kenneth Norwick:
>And then compromise?

Mr. Klein:
>If you have a model, you may not necessarily have to compromise because a lot of school boards will want a model. One of the big problems the APA had in the civil commitment area was that it had a model commitment law. It was passed on by half the state legislatures. If you have something, you've done the work for other people.

Kenneth Norwick:
>But that implies that if you offer it to them, you're playing the game. And then if they want to cut back on the appellate review process, if they want to cut back on the hearing, you're semiobligated to play the game with them.

Mr. Klein:
>Can you get more in court?

Kenneth Norwick:
>I asked you first.

Richard Schmidt:
>I would like to make a comment before we get away from the amicus thing. In the First Amendment field in the last ten years, every time a case has gone to the U.S. Supreme Court, it's been like flies around horse droppings the way the amicus briefs come in. And one of the Justices on the Supreme Court said to me, "You're all saying the same thing in a different style and if you think we're going to read that, you're crazy." I spent an entire month in getting the *Tornillo* briefs[5] ready, just writing letters of permission for other people to come in

as *amicus*. Each lawyer involved thinks he can write a better brief than the other guy. And if you think it's fun to try to coordinate an *amicus* effort, come around some time. We're crazy when we throw all that in. It's *not* read. Any clerk from any circuit court or the Supreme Court, or the judges themselves, will admit that they do not read them. And that's particularly true when you get an *amicus* brief that goes further and is more elaborate than the original brief itself.

Henry Kaufman:

Dick, are they reading *one* brief?

Richard Schmidt:

Yes, in many instances, they will. It is particularly useless, I understand, on things like petitions for *certiorari*, or petitions for rehearing, where it seems to be virtually of no value whatsoever.

Mr. Klein:

The problem is there are organizations and organizations. The Supreme Court knows that I can incorporate a dozen organizations within the next half-an-hour, each of whom has one member. There are some organizations which, if they come in—even the ACLU, despite the problems it's had in the last ten years in the Supreme Court—are recognized organizations. What I would do on petition for *certiorari* is put a two-page thing together saying these people are interested in this issue. I wouldn't give them any legal argument or anything.

Bruce Ennis:

I have a very different perspective on *amicus* briefs, particularly at the Supreme Court level. The ACLU is involved in about fifty, sometimes as many as one hundred, cases per term in the Supreme Court. The majority of those are *amicus* briefs. And I agree that it's almost a total waste of time to file a "me, too" *amicus* brief, supporting the side you want to support by simply writing a little more eloquently what the parties are already saying to the court. That's a waste of time. The kinds of *amicus* briefs we now file are directed at making points that the other parties are not making and perhaps, because of their particular clients, *cannot* make. Most of our *amicus* briefs are rather narrow and defensive because it's our perception that most of these frontline, pioneer issues are more likely to lose in the Supreme Court than to win. So what we try to do is to say to the Court, "You don't have to decide the whole universe of issues in favor of schoolchildren, in this case, in order for them to prevail. Here's a narrow ground on which you can win." Or, we say in many cases where it looks like an almost certain loser that, "You should not decide the case at all. *Certiorari* was improvidently granted, there was an independent and adequate state-law ground on which you could have based the decision." Or, "In order to decide this case, you need not resolve the following five issues, and here's one." That kind of brief, I am convinced, is very effective. We have to think in terms of what is the function of an *amicus* brief? It depends on what court you're in. If we're likely to be losing these global-type cases in the Supreme Court, then *amicus* briefs have a very important role—not to push for affirmative development of the law, but rather to hold the line so we don't lose what we've got.

Mr. Klein:

This is the ACLU model. You start out with, "This case does not raise . . ." and go on from there. "This trivial case should never have been. . . ." So there are cases where it clearly works.

Unidentified Speaker:

If the prospect of getting a satisfactory resolution at the Supreme Court level is unlikely, counsel should consider the possibility of trying to develop the law through the state courts, on state constitutional grounds. There are many state courts which would be more receptive to the type of arguments being made here than the United States Supreme Court is today. The *PruneYard* case[6] suggests that people situated as we are should really look very carefully at the possibility of developing law at the state level, even if you're writing on a clean slate. A loss at the level of a state court of last resort is going to be much less ruinous than a loss at the United States Supreme Court level. You've got a percolation effect. So five or ten years hence, when a case does get up to the Supreme Court, a counsel can point to the successful experience of various states that have adopted certain rules of law. And the arguments of counsel don't appear nearly so novel or represent such a great threat.

Richard Kleeman:

All of you are lawyers and quite understandably are arguing the strict technical value of *amicus* briefs. As a nonlawyer and an executive of the Association of American Publishers, I would like to suggest two benefits from an association point of view—namely, the education of one, the members, and two, the general public—which I don't think you get by signing onto somebody else's brief, however excellent it may be.

COMMUNICATING

Stephen Borofsky:

I'm a single practitioner from Nashua, New Hampshire, who did the *Ms.* magazine case[7] without any sort of ACLU involvement. From the federal district court point of view, and from my point of view, it's not quite clear to me whether the ACLU intends to take every First Amendment book censorship case which comes down the pike. If it doesn't, then you've got to address yourself to the rest of us who need some help in different ways than you've been talking about. I felt quite ill at ease going into the district court without a very knowledgeable idea of what the First Amendment was all about. You've got to be able to go into the district court and say, "This is a case which involves the First Amendment. You can't do it, even though it's a public school. Call it what you want, you can't censor books." It's important to address what one says to the district court judge who knows less, or only as much, as I do about the First Amendment. In the *Ms.* magazine case, the court did say that school boards, despite the authority they have and however you relate that to the First Amendment, can't ban books for political reasons. And it seems to me that when you bring a procedural type of theory, you are more likely to get the response: "Okay, remand it and we'll have to go through the procedure correctly." It's somewhat important to develop a consistent, conceptual basis for front line people to present to district court judges, so that you don't wind up with that problem.

Unidentified Speaker:

In preparing your case for trial and in proving these various theories, some of the lawyers might want to consider a technique that we're developing in some of our cases. That is one of content analysis. Content analysis, in the kinds of litigation that we're handling, is an analysis of the rhetoric which is used to support a particular action, to tie that rhetoric into a prohibited kind of motivation. There are expert witnesses who can do this kind of content analysis. A fruitful area to explore in these First Amendment censorship-type cases is to show that this particular act of censorship is tied into a local, regional, or national effort to purge a particular type of book from a library or from the public schools. The lawyers should collect all the literature they can which is related to this effort—all publications, pamphlets, and articles which relate to this campaign, particularly in the local newspapers. If there is a public debate on this kind of censorship action, letters to newspaper editors on this issue should be collected. Then submit this to an expert in content analysis. In some cases, you may be able to make an "establishment" case; you may find that the protestors don't like books with dirty words in them in the libraries or the public schools, because they belong to a religiously oriented group to which this is offensive. Therefore, you have an establishment claim, even though it's a dirty book case. You may find, or your content analysis expert may be able to demonstrate, that this is a purely ideological or political motivation. This is one technique that we can use to prove a prohibited motivation. This area might very well be worth exploring.

To assist lawyers in handling these cases—maybe this is being done already—someone should be commissioned to do a book or a paper on the national efforts to rid the public schools or libraries of certain kinds of books. If somebody would publish a book in this area, this person could testify in these cases as an expert witness and document in very specific terms the dimensions of this national effort.

Diane Shugert:

There is Ed Jenkinson. He's former chair of the Committee Against Censorship of the National Council of Teachers of English, the position which I hold. His book is called *Censors in the Classroom: The Mind Benders,* University of Southern Illinois Press.

Unidentified Speaker:

It's a good book and was published recently.

Kenneth D. McCormick:

There are dozens of such books.

Unidentified Speaker:

Jenkinson's book takes, point by point, the secular humanism approach, the books that have been under attack, obscenity cases, and so forth. He's done a lot of TV.

Judith Krug:

Lawyers handling these cases need to have a complete bibliography of all the materials which document national campaigns and local campaigns to censor these books. It's very important. There's a bibliography in each issue of the ALA *Newsletter on Intellectual Freedom,* which is the most complete, up-to-date bibliography you'll find in the area. We also reviewed Jenkinson's book when it came out.

Frank Parker:

The right-wing books in these cases are often the most revealing because it is important to analyze the campaign rhetoric. We've been doing this in some of our racial discrimination cases. People don't say anymore, "We're doing it because they're black." But they use the rhetoric of white supremacy; and we can establish motivation, even when they don't explicitly mention race, by showing that they are using white supremacy rhetoric. If you analyze their rhetoric and can tie it to some of this right-wing literature, you will be able to show political, ideological, and religious motivation in many cases. It will be very helpful, since the Supreme Court is making it increasingly difficult for us to show improper motivation. If you can use these kinds of techniques, it will enhance the proof in each of these cases.

Mr. Halpern:

It seems to me that this comment raises a larger question, and that is, How do you inform lawyers litigating these cases about what's going on so that they're in touch with all expert thinking in the field? In many public interest law areas, what you need is some kind of reporter service that is available for lawyers in the field. The *Selective Service Law Reporter;* the *Mental Health Law Reporter;* the early civil rights stuff that Tony Amsterdam did which became a bible for civil rights litigators in the sixties and early seventies; model pleading files—these are things which have been developed in other areas. That tried-and-true technique would be an extremely useful one. Another question is, Why not do things other than litigate? One thing lawyers can do is to draft model procedures for book selection. One of the things that administrative lawyers like myself train to do is to design processes. If there already are model procedures, then the lawyers ought to know about it.

Mr. Klein:

>There is another dimension of the communication problem— lawyers and judges who are trained as lawyers tend to be skeptical of experts from other disciplines. This has certainly been true in the evolution of mental health law. If you were arguing your case to judges who were trained as librarians before going on to the bench, that would be a different situation. I think it's important that librarians and lawyers talk to each other more in this area. Judges don't know that selection procedures are a matter about which there is a kind of collective judgment concerning acceptable professional procedures. Judges may think that selection of library books is a matter of reading the *New York Times Book Review* and using intuition. That is a communication gap that ought to be seriously addressed. There is a kind of science here, and it is deserving of a level of respect which I think many judges aren't going to give it.

Florence McMullin:

>All of you might consider using the ALA *Newsletter on Intellectual Freedom* as a tool; it would meet some of these needs. And I want to make a little pitch for the Freedom to Read Foundation. It disseminates information on both legislation and litigation and an ongoing record of cases and analysis to support the people out on the front line. The foundation is doing that. The office of the Freedom to Read Foundation is in Chicago.

COORDINATING

Judith Krug:

>There are attempts to coordinate that are going on at the present time. One of those efforts is the Academic Freedom Group, the AFG. The American Library Association is involved in that as are some of the other organizations that are here right now. A number of regional meetings have taken place to develop state coalitions, state AFGs—for example, the state of Utah. Utah has a recruiting list of fifty-one organizations it is trying to get involved in that state AFG. There now are twenty-two state coalitions. They are starting to move and, with your cooperation, will move in this direction. Several of the expert witnesses that we use, including Dr. Otto Larsen and Dr. Wardell Pomeroy, are subscribers to the *Newsletter on Intellectual Freedom* and they find it invaluable.

Howard Besser:

Sometimes organizations file *amicus* briefs, which may have the effect of cutting the legs out from under a litigating lawyer. It may be that an organization in its collective wisdom has decided that a litigating lawyer has proceeded inappropriately. I would suggest to my colleagues in the ACLU that it might be advisable that rather than waiting for a Supreme Court argument situation, or Supreme Court brief, that that kind of guidance might be better given at an earlier level. Not that the ACLU hasn't often given that kind of help, but quite candidly, often they have not. That's something to consider within our own ranks.

Ann Brick:

Librarians from intellectual freedom committees can be very helpful on a practical level; they can do things that the ACLU can't afford to do or doesn't have the resources to do. They did a survey for us in California of a high school library system to see how many had Richard Brautigan's books, and while I recognize that it should have been inadmissable, the judge looked at it and it was one of the things he considered.

Judith Krug:

There is a state intellectual freedom committee attached to every state library association in the nation. A telephone call to our headquarters will get you a name and address, a telephone number, and an introduction in thirty seconds. The academic freedom coalitions in each state collect newspaper clippings and the materials circulated within the schools from all sources. The national coalition has ten organizations in it. We get just about everything that's circulated in schools to back up some of these things.

FORUMS FOR LITIGATION

Alan Levine:

One comment about single-book controversies. All I can say is the obvious—that that's a less favorable situation in which to litigate. But that is sometimes unavoidable if it becomes a major public controversy. Some of the single-book cases should be avoided, if possible. That may have been part of the lesson in *Presidents Council.* Second, about the use of social scientists—I'm particularly skeptical about their effectiveness in proving a "pall," a chilling effect. I think social scientists don't have much expertise there, and I suspect they will be rebutted by equally persuasive social scientists who say there is no pall. If there is a pall of orthodoxy, evidence of it is in places like the Island Trees school system. Our talking to students there makes it perfectly clear and we'll attempt to prove it if we go back to trial. There really is a pall of orthodoxy in that school system—teachers are, as a result of what the school board did there, genuinely afraid to risk teaching or talking about controversial books. There are some cases that ought to be abandoned once you get into them, either at the district court level before you go to decision or after an unfavorable decision. Sometimes you don't have control of that. Sometimes you have a client, such as a discharged teacher, and you can't abandon the client. If it's a straight book removal and your client is really a front for organizational, social concern, then often you can have control over the case if you draft a proper retainer providing that control. Organizations don't often draft retainers. When I was with the ACLU, we rarely did, but let me commend it to you.

Last, I want to comment on the issue of state court venue that Fred Le Clercq talked about. Consider it strongly; we did in *Pico*. One of those little-known facts, unless you read the opinion carefully, is that that case was filed in state court. We had *Presidents Council* facing us in the Second Circuit, and we had at that time—and presently—a New York Court of Appeals that seemed to have a larger vision and a sense of history, and that might be looking for this kind of case. So it was our collective judgment that state court was the proper place to file that. However, sophisticated litigators that we are, we not only threw in state constitutional claims, so that the court would not be bound by the Second Circuit's opinion interpreting the First Amendment, but we threw in a First Amendment claim, in case we lost in the New York Court of Appeals and wanted to go to the Supreme Court—so that we would have federal, constitutional grounds on which to appeal. The school board lawyers then removed the case to federal court on the grounds that it presented a substantial constitutional question. We were then in the position of arguing that it did not suggest a substantial constitutional question because after all, in *Presidents Council*, the court of appeals had said the First Amendment rights here were "miniscule." The school board lawyer, however, said it did present a substantial constitutional question and that *Presidents Council* was distinguishable. The district court so held, said that *Presidents Council* didn't control, and granted removal. Then, of course, when the district court rendered its opinion, it found, after reading the briefs carefully, that *Presidents Council*, indeed, did control. The caution in that case would be that if you're going to proceed in state court, do not look ahead to the U.S. Supreme Court, and the wisdom probably would be not to allege federal constitutional grounds.

Frank Askin:

As one who has expert witnesses in a number of cases to try to prove something called chilling effect, I would particularly call everyone's attention to the Third Circuit opinion in *Paton* v. *LaPrade* a few years ago.[8] If we had not had social science affidavits on chilling effect in the record, I do not think we would have prevailed in the Third Circuit.

Let me emphasize the public education role of this kind of litigation in general and *amicus* briefs, in particular. Sometimes I think it may be more important to file *amicus* briefs in the press room than with the Justices. And I think there's some support in the *Brethren* for that kind of argument. I really would like to stress the function of litigation as a political strategy, and success as a function of something more than good judicial decisions. Perhaps the best model for this is the twelve years of political surveillance litigation in this country. In 1969, when the country's first police surveillance suit was filed in New Jersey, police surveillance of political dissidents was taken for granted. It was just assumed that police did that, that it was part of the police role. As a result of twelve years of litigation, and the surrounding political action which the litigation activities inspired, the public climate has substantially been changed in this country. People no longer agree it is the proper function of police to spy on political dissidents. The truth is there have been almost no judicial victories in this twelve-year campaign despite hundreds of cases. The judicial opinions which denounce, or cast doubt on, the legality of police surveillance of dissidents are very few and far between, for a variety of reasons. It seems to me the litigation campaign that's been waged has been amazingly successful in changing public climate and public policy in this country. But we're going to get a backlash now with the new administration unleashing the FBI and all this. So the campaign is not over. But, in fact, it seems to me that the twelve-year campaign has been extraordinarily successful without many judicial victories. And I think it's a good model to consider when we're talking about how to use litigation to accomplish this particular political end.

Henry Kaufman:

What do we think can come out of this colloquium? What should we be doing now that we have discussed the social climate, the legal background, and the litigation strategy?

THE TEACHER'S PERSPECTIVE

Diane Shugert:

Earlier, what I had learned from being at this session was that, according to what I had heard, I ought not to be here at all. Remember, I represent the English teachers. Librarians of school libraries have barely a place in court. If they have barely a place in court, teachers certainly do not have a place. When people mention the various constituencies that you might involve in these cases, teachers are not mentioned. The particular teacher, by the way, who may have been told to take the book out of the class, is not part of a real constituency. I have discovered that you do not know that we, too, have a set of professional procedures that a teacher ought to follow in choosing a work to use in class. Those procedures are published by our national council and by state councils and various organizations, and they are very widely distributed. A book that I didn't mention, *Dealing with Censorship*, edited by James Davis and published by the National Council of Teachers of English, has a series of articles including one by Ed Jenkinson, which is one of the first to appear, detailing how the Right interferes in school cases.

In that Davis book, those procedures are outlined, including long articles on an appropriate rationale for teaching a book; how to write it up; what ought to appear in it; how other people ought to be considered, besides your own professional judgment—many things that would serve to convince the court that the choice of a particular book to use in a class is not a matter of chance, not a matter of the teacher's expressing his own First Amendment right to speak his opinion. The teacher is *not* free in quite that way in the classroom, and the procedures recognize that. Those things are appropriate to discovery. I've not learned from you whether it would also be helpful for those committees that decide which procedures a school will use to include a wide variety beyond teachers and administrators, for example. If they do, does that give them greater force when someone challenges the selection of the book—if various groups are represented in actually arranging the procedures by which books are selected and by which they are challenged? It seems to me that it would help, and we're just moving to do things like that.

From the teacher's point of view, this is the big issue. You can't teach English this way. That's the issue—not that I can't express my opinion. English teachers in my state take an entire series of courses that the state requires them to take. One is called Adolescent Literature, in which the teacher learns of hundreds of books she can recommend that might excite kids about reading. The teacher who takes that course doesn't want to push any one of those books; she simply wants to get kids to read better. But if you cannot say, "Hey, you might like this book. You like to read about ships. Here's a book that has a lot of ships in it," because one of the ship captains uses God's name in vain—if you can't make that kind of recommendation to kids, then you can't teach them to read. If you're in a school that has invasion of privacy procedures, then you can't ask a kid, "Do you think this book presents a true picture of the world as you know it?" because you're invading his privacy. You can't do the thing that you're supposedly hired to do. You have talked about the school boards because they are the defendants in these cases that we bring, and you have also talked about parents or students, but where is the teacher in all that? Perhaps nowhere.

Since you have been talking about developing a body of law and getting various kinds of cooperation from organizations, we teachers are willing to cooperate on a long-term project of working first with the easiest cases—the librarians perhaps—and then moving on eventually to develop that into something that protects English itself—not the teacher. The fact is that a teacher cannot communicate to a kid that there are black poets and that the poems themselves would appeal to the kids, when some of these attacks come about. The librarian is the one who brings the suit, but the English teacher is also there under the same difficulties. And that was true in *Chelsea*, where an English teacher was one of the people who took part in the suit. The same remedies were found for the English teacher as for the librarian. Both were plaintiffs and there was testimony to establish the need, as far as the English teacher was concerned, to have available in the library the sorts of books which the school board had removed.

We teachers don't even have the pretense from the censors that the science people have. You see, the censors in our area cannot complain that there is an alternative theory. The censors who want the books out of the English classes want books out. They do not have books to put in their places;

they do not have a nice, happy book that presents God in a nice, happy way. So that's one area in which the English teacher's cases are often a little clearer than some of these other cases—it is a matter of getting a book out and there being no alternative.

Unidentified Speaker:

We are in a very early formative stage in the development of the law in this area. If we want to make a beachhead and establish the principles and win cases early, we ought to sue the goofy school board first. We should pick on the weakest defendant. With respect to developing the legal theories, as has been urged throughout this conference, there are any number of levels of analysis with which we still need to deal to reinforce the litigation strategy that we employ. If, for example, we are going to advance the pall of orthodoxy theory, does it mean some sort of environmental analysis as to whether there is in fact a pall of orthodoxy within the classroom? Or does it mean that we inquire into the motive of the school board members to find out whether they are attempting to impose a pall of orthodoxy? Even if they don't succeed, will we regard that as permissible? There are all sorts of levels of inquiry that need further exploration.

Michelle Kamhi:

In going through the state-level policies and procedures, many states have clauses going back ten, twenty, thirty years, stating that no textbook shall be used that speaks slightingly of the founding fathers, or that have subversive material in them. In the follow-up interviews, when I asked the state-level textbook officers whether any of these clauses had even been called into consideration for any adoptions, they could not recall any. But with all of the activity of the New Right, I am concerned that this might suddenly be resurrected. That might be something to keep in mind.

Diane Shugert:

The panel might regard the development of the larger picture which is a source of concern to educators who find literature and materials suffering in their local community.

What are some of the economic needs, particularly during a time of inflation and greater need for resources for private education in particular? I see two issues surfacing in terms of the impact of materials, particularly on the Right, but also to a certain extent on the Left, that need to be clarified. One is the implicit message that schools in America are somehow liberal. The other is that they do not teach the truth. There is great danger in both of these notions. Large numbers of persons within our society do not understand that education, at its best, has a regard for evidence and decency and for an understanding of pluralism within our society and not just liberalism or conservatism. We've got lots of conservative teachers, as I'm sure you know. A lot of people are susceptible to rhetoric now, and are not looking at some of the fundamental notions of what education is all about in a society. Educators cannot do it alone, librarians cannot do it alone, and perhaps the legal profession cannot do it alone. We need one another very much.

Regarding climate, it is now rather clear, in terms of the data on the future of public education, that we are going to experience a dwindling political constituency. It is clear that the enrollment in public schools is dropping, that state after state is experiencing financial hardship.

Not only are there the economic concerns and the political concerns; the very real problem I'm seeing when I talk with educators around the country is a feeling of hopelessness, that no one cares. How sad it is to hear a teacher say, "When I come back home after the class, I don't want to talk with anyone in the community. They're going to say that I'm feeding from the public trough." And there is, I think, a developing morale crisis. When you are under stress and frustration, as many teachers are, and others add even more stress and frustration, the teachers are going to say, "The hell with it. Take the book out. Do whatever you want to do. I'll put in my eight hours and hope I can retire and get out." There are indications that many of our best teachers—who've been teaching for ten, fifteen, twenty years—are leaving.

POLICIES AND PROCEDURES

David Rabban:

My question for Judy Krug and also for people representing teachers' organizations is whether you have tried or succeeded in getting conventions of understanding between your organization and school boards, for example, as to what proper procedures are.

Judith Krug:

We have a program that is in progress right now, "we" being the Intellectual Freedom Committee of the American Library Association, with the American Association of School Administrators, which is the superintendents' association in the entire country, representing approximately eighty-five percent of school superintendents. We have a three-pronged program. One is the development of board policy and procedure. Our belief, within the library profession, is that it is incumbent upon the librarians and the teachers to develop this material, these kinds of policies and procedures, but that these should be approved by the appropriate governing body. The reason we started working with AASA is because that is the power center most concerned with the education side of the question, as opposed to the school board which is on the public side of education. So we are working with superintendents all across the country in the development of these kinds of policies and procedures right now.

David Rabban:

There's a legal point behind my question. If you can get actual conventions ratified and in writing, that could provide an alternative legal theory to protect you in some of these school censorship cases. I'm speaking from our perspective in the American Association of University Professors, where we have a number of conventions with administrators. Often, in court, we can rely on those conventions as support for our principles even if constitutional law doesn't support us.

Judith Krug:

Policies and procedures are absolute imperatives for running a library. They are absolutely imperative because we're dealing with public funds, if for no other reason. So the most important reason is not intellectual freedom, but that's where we stand. That's our first line of defense. It is as close as we are going to come to what you call a convention—adopted school board procedures and policies.

David Rabban:

I am suggesting something like going to the national convention of the National Association of School Boards and getting them to adopt policies just as, for instance, our group has adopted them.

Judith Krug:
> Both of you should adopt the same policy and then go into court and say that you've both adopted this policy?

David Rabban:
> It's like a board-union agreement.

Judith Krug:
> The Minnesota School Board Association did adopt a statement vis-a-vis policies and procedures for the selection of school curricular and school library materials. That's the only state that has a state-level policy. And that's about as far as we're going to be able to go. I don't think that we really want a national policy; it's going to be too diluted.

SUMMING UP

Florence McMullin:
> Before all the litigators get away, as a client from the Freedom to Read Foundation, I have a little laundry list here. This is also for the organizers of the colloquium. It would really be valuable for all of us if there was a published report of this meeting. It has been a really inspiring interaction and exchange and I would certainly like to see it going out to a wider audience. I hope that there will be a continued dialogue among these groups. Things are continually happening and changing. I would like to see increased attention to legislation violating First Amendment rights, along with political awareness. The courtroom, you know, is not the only arena in which to defend the First Amendment. It would really be valuable if you would all share whatever effective methods you do develop. We would like to see practical, innovative strategies to meet the increasingly sophisticated pressures on librarians and libraries. We'd like to keep the librarians on the job. We'd like to keep the books on the open shelves and in circulation. And we really want you to make good law. Do that for us because we feel that the law and censorship are going to be here a whole lot longer than any of us.

Burton Joseph:
> On behalf of the sponsoring organizations, thank you all for making this colloquium possible.

Summaries of Major Cases

TINKER v. DES MOINES INDEPENDENT COMMUNITY
SCHOOL DISTRICT, 393 U.S. 503 (1969)

The *Tinker* case arose when a group of students decided to publicize their objection to the Vietnam war and their support for a truce by wearing black armbands in school during the 1967 holiday season. When the principals of the Des Moines schools became aware of the students' intentions, they announced that any student wearing an armband would be asked to remove it and if the request were refused, the student would be suspended until he or she returned without the armband.

A number of students, among them John and Mary Beth Tinker and Christopher Eckhardt (fifteen, thirteen, and sixteen, respectively), went ahead with their plans and wore the armbands to school. There was no disturbance or disruption of normal school activities, but nevertheless, the students were told to remove their armbands in accordance with the principals' edict. When they refused, they were ordered to leave school. They returned to school two weeks later, sans armbands, but in the meantime, had filed suit in federal court.

The Tinkers and Eckhardt lost their case at both the district court level and in the United States Court of Appeals. The U.S. Supreme Court, however, reversed these decisions. The majority opinion pointed out in February 1969 that neither students nor teachers "shed their Constitutional right to freedom of speech or expression at the schoolhouse gate." The Court held that the First Amendment protects the rights of public school children to express their political and social views during school hours. The decision held further that school officials may not place arbitrary curbs on student speech in the public schools. It is particularly interesting to note that while many individuals had taken for granted that school children did have First Amendment rights of free speech, the Supreme Court had never directly said so prior to this case.

PRESIDENTS COUNCIL, DISTRICT 25 v. COMMUNITY SCHOOL BOARD NO. 25 (NEW YORK CITY), 457 F.2d 289, (2d Cir. 1972), 409 U.S. 998 (1972)

This 1972 case was the first to consider whether a school board could remove books from a school library. At issue was a school board action revoking library access by junior high school students to *Down These Mean Streets*, by Piri Thomas, an autobiographical account of a Puerto Rican growing up in Spanish Harlem. The book's language and graphic sexual scenes offended some people in the community, who requested its removal.

The opinion of the U.S. Court of Appeals for the Second Circuit reflected the traditional deference to school board discretion by upholding its action revoking free access to Thomas' novel. Bypassing the constitutional aspects of the case, the court reduced the issue to one of shelving a book: "To suggest that the shelving or unshelving of books presents a constitutional issue, particularly when there is no showing of a curtailment of freedom of speech or thought, is a proposition we cannot accept." Judge Mulligan, writing for the court, declared that someone has to bear responsibility for book selection, and since school boards are statutorily empowered to operate the schools and prescribe the curriculum, the board is the appropriate body.

MINARCINI v. STRONGSVILLE (OHIO) CITY SCHOOL DISTRICT, 541 F.2d 577 (6th Cir. 1976)

This suit was prompted by the Strongsville City Board of Education's rejection of faculty recommendations to approve the purchase of Joseph Heller's *Catch-22* and Kurt Vonnegut's *God Bless You, Mr. Rosewater* for use in the high school curriculum. The school board also ordered two books, *Catch-22* and Vonnegut's *Cat's Cradle*, removed from the library. No official reason was given for the removal; the only apparent explanation was contained in the minutes of a board meeting at which the books were described as "completely sick" and "garbage."

In 1976 the U.S. Court of Appeals for the Sixth Circuit ruled against the school board, upholding the students' First Amendment right to receive information and the librarians' right to disseminate it. Judge Edward, writing for the court, rejected the absolute right of a school board to remove from the library any book it might regard with disfavor:

> A library is a storehouse of knowledge. When created for a public school, it is an important privilege created by the state for the benefit of students in the schools. That privilege is not subject to being withdrawn by succeeding school boards whose

members might desire to "winnow" the library for books the contents of which occasioned their displeasure or disapproval.

The court further emphasized that the responsibility of the board to provide access to material could not be minimized by the availability of the books in sources outside the school.

RIGHT TO READ DEFENSE COMMITTEE v. SCHOOL COMMITTEE OF THE CITY OF CHELSEA, 454 F. Supp. 703 (D. Mass. 1978)

In 1976, the banning of a poetry anthology, *Male and Female under 18*, by the Chelsea (Massachusetts) School Committee was challenged in federal court. Plaintiffs were Chelsea school librarian Sonja Coleman and a group organized to support her, the Right to Read Defense Committee of Chelsea.

The action against *Male and Female under 18* reflected the school committee's strong dislike of one poem in the anthology, "The City to a Young Girl," by Jody Caravaglia.

The school committee argued that under Massachusetts law the school committee has clear authority to approve or disapprove works used in the schools. In addition, the committee argued that they had legally decided not to include sex education in the curriculum and that "The City to a Young Girl" represented an effort to introduce the subject improperly.

The Right to Read Defense Committee contended that *Male and Female under 18* is fully protected by the First Amendment, that students possess a right to have access to materials fully protected by the First Amendment, and that the school committee's objections to the poem as "vulgar and offensive" could not constitutionally justify its suppression.

In July 1978, U.S. District Judge Joseph L. Tauro enjoined the school committee "from removing, or causing to be removed, in whole or in part," the anthology, which was to be made available to students "in accordance with standard library procedures." Relying particularly on the *Minarcini* precedent, Judge Tauro held that the committee's attempt to ban "The City to a Young Girl" could not pass First Amendment standards established by Supreme Court and lower court rulings.

PICO v. BOARD OF EDUCATION, ISLAND TREES, 474 F. Supp. 387 (E.D.N.Y. 1979), 638 F.2d 404 (2d Cir. 1980), 457 U.S.—(1982)

In 1976, the school board removed nine books from the library shelves of the Island Trees Union Free School District in Long Island, New York.

The books were *The Fixer, Slaughterhouse-Five, Soul on Ice, The Naked Ape, Down These Mean Streets, Best Short Stories by Negro Writers, Go Ask Alice, A Hero Ain't Nothin' but a Sandwich,* and *A Reader for Writers.* The books were banned after three members of the school board attended a meeting of conservative parents at which a list of "objectionable" books was distributed.

In August 1979, U.S. District Court Judge George C. Pratt ruled in favor of the school board, saying that it is legitimate for school boards to examine school library materials in order to determine their "suitability." Relying heavily on the precedent of the *Presidents Council* case, Judge Pratt ruled that the First Amendment rights of the student plaintiffs had not been violated:

> ... the Island Trees school board removed certain books because it viewed them as vulgar and in bad taste, a removal that clearly was content based. Whether they were correct in their evaluation of the books is not the issue.

> ... the issue is whether the First Amendment requires a federal court to forbid a school board from removing library books which its members find to be inconsistent with the basic values of the community that elected them.

> ... In the absence of a sharp, focused issue of academic freedom, the court concludes that respect for the traditional values of the community and deference to the school board's substantial control over educational content preclude any finding of a First Amendment violation ...

In October 1980, the U.S. Court of Appeals for the Second Circuit reversed the lower court decision and held that the student plaintiffs had stated a sustainable claim for violation of First Amendment rights. The three-judge panel, which divided two to one, did not enter final judgment in the students' favor but instead remanded the case for trial. The court held that the criteria for the removal of the books were too general and overbroad.

In 1981, in response to a request for *certiorari* from the school board, the Supreme Court agreed to review the case. In June 1982, the Supreme Court remanded the case to federal district court. The decision was badly split, but the plurality opinion argued that the case should be tried in order to discover whether the school board had acted to inhibit the spread of ideas with which it disagreed, which could violate First Amendment rights of students, or, in contrast, had removed the books because they were pervasively vulgar. The opinion opposes the suppression of ideas in the high school library. The concurring Justice, while not sharing this opinion, noted that the case should be tried because of the unresolved issue of the reason underlying the school board's removal of the books.

BICKNELL v. VERGENNES UNION HIGH SCHOOL BOARD, 475 F. Supp. 615 (D. Vt. 1979), 638 F.2d 438 (2d Cir. 1980)

In this Vermont case litigated in 1979, U.S. District Court Judge Albert W. Coffin dismissed a complaint filed by librarian Elizabeth Phillips, several students, and others to protest the board's removal of *The Wanderers* and *Dog Day Afternoon* from the library; the imposition of a freeze on new library acquisitions; and the board's policy of screening all major acquisitions.

The court held that school boards have final authority in such matters and that the restrictions did not violate the constitutional rights of students or librarians:

> Although the court does not entirely agree with the policies and actions of the defendants we do not find that those policies and actions directly or sharply infringe upon the basic constitutional rights of the students of Vergennes Union High School.
>
> . . . the detailed procedures set forth for removing works from the collection obviously condition the general statements of the rights of those persons affected by the policy. Furthermore, the right of professional personnel under that policy "to freely select" materials for the collection are explicitly limited by the phrase "in accordance with Board policy."

In October 1980, the United States Court of Appeals for the Second Circuit, in a two to one decision, affirmed the dismissal.

LOEWEN v. TURNIPSEED, 488 F. Supp. 1138 (N.D. Miss. 1980)

A ninth-grade history textbook, *Mississippi: Conflict and Change*, by James W. Loewen and Charles Sallis, became a subject of controversy in 1974 when the Mississippi Textbook Purchasing Board refused to approve it for use in Mississippi public schools. The textbook committee, which can approve up to five history texts, selected only a revised version of the book used in ninth-grade classrooms in Mississippi for nearly two decades.

Loewen charged that the approved book "stigmatizes black people" and fails to mention or gives only passing reference to renowned Mississippi blacks. The five white members of the textbook committee rejected *Conflict and Change* on the grounds that it was too concerned with racial matters and too controversial; the two black members of the committee judged it suitable.

A suit was brought before U.S. District Judge Orma R. Smith, who ruled that the criteria used for selecting textbooks by the Mississippi committee were not justifiable grounds for rejecting *Mississippi: Conflict and Change*. Judge Smith held that because the controversial racial material in the book was a factor leading to its rejection, the plaintiff authors had been denied their constitutionally guaranteed rights of freedom of speech and of the press.

ZYKAN v. WARSAW (INDIANA) COMMUNITY SCHOOL CORPORATION AND WARSAW SCHOOL BOARD OF TRUSTEES, 631 F.2d 1300 (7th Cir. 1980)

At issue was a curriculum review conducted by the school board in 1977, which resulted in the discontinuance of certain courses, the removal of certain courses, the removal of some books from the curriculum, the dismissal of several teachers, and the discontinuance of publication of the high school newspaper. A high school student brought suit seeking to reverse school officials' decision to "limit or prohibit the use of certain textbooks, to remove a certain book from the school library, and to delete certain courses from the curriculum."

The district court dismissed Zykan's suit, which charged that school officials had violated constitutional guarantees of academic freedom and the "right to know." The case was then appealed to the U.S. Court of Appeals for the Seventh Circuit, which ruled that the school board has the right to establish a curriculum on the basis of its own discretion, but that it is forbidden to impose a "pall of orthodoxy" on the classroom. The right of students to file legal complaints about the school curriculum was recognized; however, the court held that the claims of students "must cross a relatively high threshold before entering upon the field of a constitutional claim suitable for federal court litigation."

NOTES

FOREWORD

1. Zykan v. Warsaw Community School Corp., 631 F.2d 1300 (7th Cir. 1980).
2. Pico v. Board of Education, Island Trees, 474 F. Supp. 387 (E.D.N.Y. 1979), rev'd, 638 F.2d 404 (2d Cir. 1980).
3. Bicknell v. Vergennes Union High School, 475 F. Supp. 615 (D. Vt. 1979), aff'd, 638 F.2d 438 (2d Cir. 1980).

CURRENT SOCIAL AND POLITICAL TRENDS

1. Presidents Council, District 25 v. Community School Board No. 25, 457 F.2d 289 (2d Cir. 1972).
2. Rosenberg v. Board of Education, 196 Misc. 542, 92 N.Y. Supp. 2d 344 (1949).
3. Parker v. Board of Education, 237 F. Supp. 222 (D. Md.) aff'd, 348 F.2d 464 (4th Cir. 1965), cert denied, 382 U.S. 1030 (1966).
4. Presidents Council, District 25 v. Community School Board No. 25, 409 U.S. 998 (1972).
5. Minarcini v. Strongsville City School District, 541 F.2d 577 (6th Cir. 1976).
6. Salvail v. Nashua Board of Education, 469 F. Supp. 1269 (D.N.H. 1979).
7. Right to Read Defense Committee v. School Committee of the City of Chelsea, 454 F. Supp. 703 (D. Mass. 1978).
8. Zykan v. Warsaw Community School Corp., 631 F.2d 1300 (7th Cir. 1980).
9. Pico v. Board of Education, 474 F. Supp. 387 (E.D.N.Y. 1979), rev'd, 638 F.2d 404 (2d Cir. 1980).
10. Bicknell v. Vergennes Union High School Board of Directors, 475 F. Supp. 615 (D. Vt. 1979), aff'd, 638 F.2d 438 (2d Cir. 1980).
11. Two recent and helpful comments reflecting this relationship are Note, Schoolbooks, School Boards, and the Constitution, 80 COLUM. L. REV. 1092 (1980); and Note, Challenging Ideological Exclusion of Curriculum Material: Rights of Students and Parents, 14 HARVARD CIVIL RIGHTS-CIVIL LIBERTIES L. REV. 485 (1979).

12. See, e.g., "Publishing: Isms in Childrens' Books," N.Y. Times, Jan. 2, 1981, p. C15.

13. Newsletter on Intellectual Freedom, Sept., 1976, p. 116.

14. Id., May 1977, p. 71.

15. Id., Sept. 1976, p. 116.

16. Kramer v. Scioto-Darby School Dist., Civil Action 72-406, S.D. Ohio, March 8, 1974.

17. Williams v. Board of Education, 388 F. Supp. 93 (S.D. W. Va. 1975), aff'd, 530 F.2d 972 (4th Cir. 1975).

18. Wright v. Houston Independent School District, 366 F. Supp. 1208, (S.D. Tex. 1972), aff'd, 486 F.2d 137 (5th Cir. 1973), cert denied, 417 U.S. 969 (1974).

19. Hendren v. Campbell, 45 U.S.L. Week 2530 (Marion City. Supr. Ct. April 14, 1977). See also Daniel v. Waters, 515 F.2d 485 (6th Cir. 1975); Steele v. Waters, 527 S.W.2d 72 (Tenn. 1975).

20. Loewen v. Turnipseed, 488 F. Supp. 1138 (N.D. Miss. 1980).

21. See Comment, Sex Discrimination: The Textbook Case, 62 CALIF. L. REV. 1312 (1974).

22. Cary v. Board of Education, 427 F. Supp. 945 (D. Colo. 1978), aff'd on different grounds, 598 F.2d 535 (10th Cir. 1979).

23. Epperson v. Arkansas, 393 U.S. 97, 104 (1968).

24. Ambach v. Norwick, 441 U.S. 68 (1979).

25. Epperson v. Arkansas, 393 U.S. 97, 111 (1968).

26. Id. at 116.

27. Cary v. Board of Education, 427 F. Supp. 945 (D. Colo. 1978).

28. Bicknell v. Vergennes Union High School Board of Directors, 475 F. Supp. 615 (D. Vt. 1979).

29. See O'Neil, Libraries, Liberties, and the First Amendment, 42 CINCINNATI L. REV. 209 (1973).

30. Goldstein, The Asserted Constitutional Right of Teachers to Determine What They Teach, 124 U. PA. L. REV. 1293 (1976).

31. Cary v. Board of Education, 427 F. Supp. 945 (D. Colo. 1978).

GENERAL DIRECTIONS OF FUTURE LITIGATION

1. National Socialist Party of America v. Village of Skokie, 432 U.S. 43 (1977), on remand, 366 N.E.2d 347 (Ill. App. 1977), application denied, 434 U.S. 1327 (1977), aff'd in part, rev'd in part, 373 N.E.2d (1978).

2. Pico v. Board of Education, Island Trees, 638 F.2d 404 (2d Cir. 1980).

3. Tinker v. Des Moines Independent Community School District, 393 U.S. 503 (1969).

4. James v. Board of Education, 461 F.2d 566 (2d Cir. 1972).

5. Moore v. Younger, L.A. Supr. Ct. C85493, 13 Jan. 1975.

6. 390 U.S. 629 (1968).

7. Fogarty v. Atchley, a civil action in the United States District Court in the District of Idaho.

8. Hendren v. Campbell, 45 U.S.L.W. 2530 (Marion City Supr. Ct. 14 April 1977).

9. Malnak v. Yogi, 440 F. Supp. 1284 (D.N.J. 1977), aff'd 592 F.2d 197 (3d Cir. 1979).

10. Wiley v. Franklin, 468 F. Supp. 133 (E.D. Tenn. 1979), modified 474 F. Supp. 525 (E.D. Tenn. 1979).

11. School District of Abington v. Schempp, 374 U.S. 203 (1963).

12. Murray v. Curlett, consolidated with *Schempp, supra,* 374 U.S. 203.

13. Cary v. Board of Education, 427 F. Supp. 945 (D.Colo. 1978).

14. Searle v. Regents of the University of California, 23 Cal 3d 448, 100 Cal Rep 194 (1972).

THE STATE AS EDITOR OR CENSOR

1. THE PUBLIC AGENDA FOUNDATION, THE SPEAKER AND THE LISTENER: A PUBLIC PERSPECTIVE ON FREEDOM OF EXPRESSION 8 (1980).

2. Id.

3. See, e.g, T. VAN GEEL, AUTHORITY TO CONTROL THE SCHOOL PROGRAM (1977); F. WIRT AND M. KIRST, THE POLITICAL WEB OF AMERICAN SCHOOLS (1972); F. FITZGERALD, AMERICA REVISED (1979); E. M. ROOT, BRAINWASHING IN THE HIGH SCHOOL (1958); O'Neil, *Libraries, Liberties, and the First Amendment,* 42 CIN. L. REV. 209 (1973).

4. See, e.g., Wisconsin v. Yoder, 406 U.S. 205 (1972); Farrington v. Toku-shigue, 273 U.S. 284 (1927). See generally Arons, *The Separation of School and State: Pierce Reconsidered,* 46 HARV. L. REV. 76 (1976); Moskowitz, *Parental Rights and State Education,* 50 WASH. L. REV. 623 (1975).

5. See, e.g., O'Neil, note 3 *supra;* Van Alstyne, *The Constitutional Rights of Teachers and Professions,* 1970 DUKE L. J. 841; Goldstein, *The Asserted Constitutional Right of Public School Teachers to Determine What They Teach,* 124 U. PA. L. REV. 1293 (1976).

6. See, e.g., O'Neil, note 3 *supra,* at 216-39; Nahmod, *First Amendment Protection for Learning and Teaching: The Scope of Judicial Review,* 18 WAYNE L. REV. 1479 (1972); Note, *First Amendment-Right to Receive Information,* 55 TEX. L. REV. 511 (1977). Compare Hirschoff, *Parents and the Public School Curriculum: Is There a Right to Have One's Child Excused from Objectionable Instruction?,* 50 S. CAL. L. REV. 871 (1977).

7. D. BOORSTIN, DEMOCRACY AND ITS DISCONTENTS 10 (1975).

8. Yudof, *When Governments Speak: Toward a Theory of Government Expression and the First Amendment,* 57 TEX. L. REV. 863 (1979) (hereinafter *When Governments Speak*). See also Shiffrin, *Government Speech,* 27 U.C.L.A. L. REV. 565, 647-53 (1980); Kamenshine, *The First Amendment's Implied Political Establishment Clause,* 67 CALIF. L. REV. 1104 (1979). See generally M. YUDOF, WHEN GOVERNMENT SPEAKS: LAW, POLITICS, AND GOVERNMENT EXPRESSION IN AMERICA (University of California Press, 1982).

9. But see J. TUSSMAN, GOVERNMENT AND THE MIND (1977).

10. J. DE MAISTRE, ON GOD AND SOCIETY 30 (1959).

11. E. ARONSON, THE SOCIAL ANIMAL 55 (1972).

12. R. M. HARE, DECISIONS OF PRINCIPLE, IN PHILOSOPHY AND EDUCATION 72, 85 (I. Scheffler, ed. 1958). See also A. N. WHITEHEAD, SCIENCE AND THE MODERN WORLD (1962).

13. See generally I. BERLIN, FOUR ESSAYS ON LIBERTY LIV (1969).

14. R. BENEDICT, PATTERNS OF CULTURE 219 (1960).

15. See generally R. M. UNGER, KNOWLEDGE AND POLITICS (1975); B. MALINOWSKI, FREEDOM AND CIVILIZATION 319-20 (1964).

16. See, e.g., Arons, note 4 supra; J. COONS AND S. SUGARMAN, EDUCATION BY CHOICE: THE CASE FOR FAMILY CONTROL (1978); Sugarman and Kirp, Rethinking Collective Responsibility for Education, 39 LAW & CONTEMP. PROB. 144 (1975). See generally R. MNOOKIN, CHILD, FAMILY, AND STATE (1978).

17. Zykan v. Warsaw Community School Corp., 631 F.2d 1300, 1304, 1305 (7th Cir. 1980), citing, inter alia, Ambach v. Norwick, 441 U.S. 68 (1979); James v. Board of Education, 461 F.2d 566 (2d Cir. 1972); Carey v. Board of Education, 598 F.2d 535 (10th Cir. 1979); Presidents Council, District 25 v. Community School Board, 457 F.2d 289 (2d Cir. 1972). See also Epperson v. Arkansas, 393 U.S. 97, 104 (1968); Pico v. Board of Education, 638 F.2d 404 (2d Cir. 1980).

18. See Stern, Challenging Ideological Exclusion of Curriculum Material: Rights of Students and Parents, 14 HARV. C. R.-CIV. LIB. L. REV. 485 (1979); Kamenshine, note 8 supra.

19. See Buckel v. Prentice, 572 F.2d 141 (6th Cir. 1978). But cf. Bonner-Lyons v. School Committee, 480 F.2d 442 (1st Cir. 1973). See generally When Governments Speak, note 8 supra.

20. Canby, The First Amendment and the State as Editor: Implications for Public Broadcasting, 52 TEX. L. REV. 1123 (1974).

21. But see Columbia Broadcasting System, Inc. v. Democratic National Committee, 412 U.S. 94 (1973) (Douglas, J.) (dicta).

22. See generally Canby note 21 supra; Garvey, Children and the First Amendment, 57 TEX. L. REV. 321 (1979).

23. Cf. FCC v. Pacifica Foundation, 438 U.S. 726 (1978); Lehman v. City of Shaker Heights, 418 U.S. 298, 306-07 (1974) (Douglas, J., concurring). See generally Black, He Cannot Choose But Hear: The Plight of the Captive Auditor, 53 COLUM. L. REV. 960 (1953).

24. Shiffrin, note 8 supra.

25. See When Governments Speak, note 8 supra, at 886-88.

26. See Tinker v. Des Moines Independent Community School District, 393 U.S. 503 (1969).

27. Id. See generally Shiffrin, note 8 supra, at 574, citing Grayned v. City of Rockford, 408 U.S. 104, 116 (1972).

28. See, e.g., Minarcini v. Strongville City School Dist., 541 F.2d 577 (6th Cir. 1976); Salvail v. Nashua Board of Education, 469 F. Supp. 1269 (D.N.H. 1979). See generally Emerson, Legal Foundations of the Right to Know, 1976 WASH. U. L. Q. 1; Gellhorn, The Right to Know: First Amendment Overbreadth? 1976 WASH. U.L.Q. 25.

29. See, e.g., Bates v. State Bar of Arizona, 433 U.S. 350 (1977); Virginia State Board of Pharmacy v. Virginia Citizens Consumer Council, Inc., 425 U.S. 748 (1976); Procunier v. Matinez, 416 U.S. 396 (1974).

30. When Governments Speak, note 8 supra, at 868.

31. See Pico v. Board of Education, 638 F.2d 404 (2d Cir. 1980). But cf. Loewen v. Turnipseed, 488 F. Supp. 1138, 1153-54 (N.D. Miss. 1980).

32. See Advocates for the Arts v. Thomson, 532 F.2d 792 (1st Cir. 1976); Close v. Lederle, 424 F.2d 988 (1st Cir. 1970). See generally Shiffrin, note 8 supra, at 640-47.

33. See Shiffrin, note 8 supra, at 640-47.

34. See generally Monaghan, *First Amendment "Due Process,"* 83 HARV. L. REV. 518 (1970).

35. See *When Governments Speak,* note 8 *supra;* Shiffrin, note 8 *supra.*

36. Shiffrin, note 8 *supra,* at 595 n.154; *When Governments Speak,* note 8 *supra,* at 872.

37. See generally M. YUDOF, WHEN GOVERNMENT SPEAKS: LAW, POLITICS, AND GOVERNMENT EXPRESSION IN AMERICA (University of California Press, 1982).

38. West Virginia State Board of Education v. Barnette, 319 U.S. 624 (1943).

39. See, e.g., Keefe v. Geanakos, 418 F.2d 359 (1st Cir. 1969); Parducci v. Rutland, 316 F. Supp. 352 (M.D. Ala. 1970).

40. See Goldstein, note 5 *supra;* Van den Haag, *Academic Freedom in the United States,* 28 LAW & CONTEMP. PROB. 515 (1963).

41. See, e.g., Keyishian v. Board of Regents, 385 U.S. 589, 603 (1967); Shelton v. Tucker, 364 U.S. 479, 487 (1960). See generally T. EMERSON, THE SYSTEM OF FREEDOM OF EXPRESSION 593-626 (1970).

42. See Goldstein, note 5 *supra,* at 1336-37.

43. *When Governments Speak,* note 8 *supra.*

44. See Yudof, note 37 *supra.*

45. Cf. Bicknell v. Vergennes Union High School Board, 638 F.2d 438 (2d Cir. 1980).

46. See, e.g., Joyner v. Whiting, 477 F.2d 456 (4th Cir. 1973); Quarterman v. Byrd, 453 F.2d 54 (4th Cir. 1971); Panarella v. Birenbaum, 32 N.Y.2d 108, 296 N.E.2d 238, 343 N.Y.S.2d 333 (1973). See generally M. YUDOF, D. KIRP, T. VAN GEEL, AND B. LEVIN, EDUCATIONAL POLICY AND THE LAW (2nd ed. 1981).

47. But see INSTITUTE OF JUDICIAL ADMINISTRATION, JUVENILE JUSTICE STANDARDS PROJECT, STANDARDS RELATING TO SCHOOL AND EDUCATION 91-4 (American Bar Association, 1977).

48. 316 F. Supp. 352 (M.D. Ala. 1970).

49. 498 F.2d 535 (10th Cir. 1979).

50. Id. at 541.

51. But see Bicknell v. Vergennes Union High School Board, 638 F.2d 438 (2d Cir. 1980).

52. See, e.g., Vitarelli v. Seaton, 359 U.S. 535 (1959); Service v. Dulles, 354 U.S. 363 (1957). Cf. United States v. Nixon, 418 U.S. 683, 695-96 (1974).

53. Monaghan, *First Amendment "Due Process,"* 83 HARV. L. REV. 518 (1970). See, e.g., Freedman v. Maryland, 380 U.S. 51 (1965); Marcus v. A Search Warrant of Property, 367 U.S. 717 (1961). See generally L. TRIBE, AMERICAN CONSTITUTIONAL LAW §12-36 (1978).

54. Cf. United States v. Nixon, 418 U.S. 683 (1974).

55. Cf. Pico v. Board of Education, 638 F.2d 404 (2d Cir. 1980).

56. Cary v. Board of Education, 598 F.2d 535 (10th Cir. 1979).

57. Id. at 544.

58. Id. at 539.

59. Id. at 538.

60. Id. at 543.

61. 469 F. Supp. 1269 (D.N.H. 1979).

62. But see Bicknell v. Vergennes Union High School Board, 638 F.2d 438 (2d Cir. 1980).

63. 469 F. Supp. at 1271.

64. Id.

65. Id. at 1273.

66. Id. at 1274. See also Pico v. Board of Education, 638 F.2d 404 (2d Cir. 1980).

67. 488 F. Supp. 1138 (N.D. Miss. 1980). But see Bicknell v. Vergennes Union High School Board, 638 F.2d 438 (2d Cir. 1980).

68. Id. at 1154.

69. Id. at 1153.

70. See generally Friendly, *Some Kind of Hearing*, 123 U. PA. L. REV. 1267 (1975).

71. See Monaghan, note 53 *supra*.

72. Compare Freedman v. Maryland, 380 U.S. 51 (1968), with Mitchell v. W. T. Grant, 416 U.S. 600 (1974).

73. Wisconsin v. Constantineau, 400 U.S. 433 (1971).

74. Paul v. Davis, 424 U.S. 693, 701 (1976). See generally L. TRIBE, AMERICAN CONSTITUTIONAL LAW §10-11 (1978).

75. See Tribe, note 74 *supra*, at §10-11.

76. M. YUDOF, WHEN GOVERNMENT SPEAKS: LAW, POLITICS, AND GOVERNMENT EXPRESSION IN AMERICA (University of California Press, 1982).

77. 488 F. Supp. at 1155.

78. As Professor Tribe has explained structural due process,

> We may begin by observing that all . . . of the constitutional models thus far examined have been concerned with ways of achieving substantive ends through variations in governmental structures and processes of choice.
>
> [A structural justice] . . . model [is] concerned [with] . . . match[ing] decision structures with substantive human ends. . . .
>
> . . . I mean [then] the approach to constitutional values that either mandates or at least favors the use of particular decisional structures for specific substantive purposes in concrete contexts, without drawing any single generalization about which decisional pattern is best suited, on the whole, to which substantive aims.

Tribe, *The Emerging Reconnection of Individual Rights and Institutional Design: Federalism, Bureaucracy, and Due Process of Lawmaking*, 10 CREIGHTON L. REV. 433, 440-41 (1977). See also Linde, *Due Process of Lawmaking*, 55 NEB. L. REV. 197 (1976). See, e.g., Panama Ref. Co. v. Ryan, 293 U.S. 388 (1935); Hampton v. Mow Sun Wong, 426 U.S. 88 (1976).

79. See, e.g., Paris Adult Theatre I v. Slaton, 413 U.S. 49 (1973).

80. See San Antonio Ind. School Dist. v. Rodriguez, 411 U.S. 1 (1973).

81. See Village of Belle Terre v. Boraas, 416 U.S. 1 (1974). Compare id. with Moore v. City of East Cleveland, 431 U.S. 494 (1977).

82. See generally L. TRIBE, AMERICAN CONSTITUTIONAL LAW 974-990 (1978).

83. See, e.g., Pico v. Board of Education, 638 F.2d 404 (2d Cir. 1980); Bicknell v. Vergennes Union High School Board, 638 F.2d 438 (2d Cir. 1980); Zykan v. Warsaw Community School Corp., 631 F.2d 1300 (7th Cir. 1980); Cary v. Board of Education, 598 F.2d 535 (10th Cir. 1979); Minarcini v. Strongsville City School Dist., 541 F.2d 577 (6th Cir. 1976); Loewen v. Turnipseed, 488 F. Supp. 1138 (N.D. Miss. 1980); Salvail v. Nashua Board of Education, 469 F. Supp. 1269

(D.N.H. 1979). But see Presidents Council, District 25 v. Community School Board, 457 F.2d 289 (2d Cir. 1972). See generally Garvey, *Children and the First Amendment*, 57 TEX. L. REV. 321 (1979).

84. *When Governments Speak*, note 8 *supra*, at 898-906, 911-12.

85. Shiffrin, note 8 *supra*.

86. See cases cited in note 83 *supra*.

87. Zykan v. Warsaw Community School Corp., 631 F.2d 1300, 1306 (7th Cir. 1980).

88. Id. at 1308-9.

89. Id. at 1302-3.

90. Id. at 1306.

91. Id.

92. See id. at 1309 (Swygert, concurring in the judgment in part).

93. Id.

94. See also Bicknell v. Vergennes Union High School Board, 638 F.2d 438, n.6 (2d Cir. 1980) (Opinion of Newman, J.).

95. See Garvey, note 83 *supra*, at 371-72.

96. Minarcini v. Strongsville City School Dist., 541 F.2d 577 (6th Cir. 1976). See also Right to Read Defense Committee of Chelsea v. School Committee of the City of Chelsea, 454 F. Supp. 703 (D. Mass. 1978).

97. See Simon, *Racially Prejudiced Governmental Actions: A Motivation Theory of the Constitutional Ban against Racial Discrimination*, 15 SAN DIEGO L. REV. 1041 (1978).

98. Cf. Mt. Healthy City School District v. Doyle, 429 U.S. 274 (1977).

99. Cf. DWORKIN, SOCIAL SCIENCES AND CONSTITUTIONAL RIGHTS: THE CONSEQUENCES OF UNCERTAINTY, IN EDUCATION, SOCIAL SCIENCE, AND THE JUDICIAL PROCESS 20 (R. Rist and R. Anson, eds. 1977).

100. 638 F.2d 404 (2d Cir. 1980).

101. 638 F.2d 438 (2d Cir. 1980).

102. Id.

103. 638 F.2d 438 (2d Cir. 1980).

104. 598 F.2d 535.

105. See *When Governments Speak*, note 8 *supra*.

106. 638 F.2d 438 (2d Cir. 1980).

107. 488 F. Supp. 1138.

108. See Board of Curators, University of Missouri v. Horowitz, 435 U.S. 78, 92n.8 (1978) ("Both Service [v. Dulles, 354 U.S. 363 (1957)] and Accardi v. Shaughnessy, 347 U.S. 260 (1954) . . . enunciate principles of federal administrative law rather than of constitutional law binding upon the States."). But cf. United States v. Nixon, 418 U.S. 683 (1974).

109. See, e.g., Paul v. Davis, 424 U.S. 693 (1976); Meachum v. Fano, 427 U.S. 215 (1976); Codd v. Velger, 429 U.S. 624 (1977); Bishop v. Wood, 426 U.S. 341 (1976). But see Goss v. Lopez, 419 U.S. 565 (1975). See generally Monaghan, *Of "Liberty" and "Property,"* 62 CORNELL L. REV. 405 (1977); Van Alstyne, *Cracks in "the New Property": Adjudicative Due Process in the Administrative State*, 62 CORNELL L. REV. 445 (1977)

110. See, e.g., Codd v. Velger, 429 U.S. 624 (1977); Carey v. Piphus, 435 U.S. 247 (1978); Mt. Healthy City School Dist. v. Doyle, 429 U.S. 274 (1977).

111. See note 78 *supra*.

112. 454 F. Supp. 703 (D. Mass. 1978).

113. Id. at 711.

114. See generally M. Yudof, When Government Speaks: Law, Politics, and Government Expression in America (University of California Press, 1982).

CURRENT LAW, FUTURE LEGAL THEORIES

1. Loewen v. Turnipseed, 488 F. Supp. 1138 (N.D. Miss. 1980).

2. See Friendly, Some Kind of Hearing, 123 U. Pa. L. Rev. 1267 (1979).

3. Village of Belle Terre v. Boraas, 416 U.S. 1 (1974).

4. Wisconsin v. Yoder, 406 U.S. 205 (1972).

5. Zykan v. Warsaw Community School Corp., 631 F.2d 1300 (7th Cir. 1980).

6. Pico v. Board of Education, Island Trees Union Free School District No. 26, 638 F.2d 404 (2d Cir. 1980).

7. Bicknell v. Vergennes Union High School Board of Directors, 638 F.2d 438 (2d Cir. 1980).

8. School District of Abington Township v. Schempp, 374 U.S. 203 (1963).

9. 319 U.S. 624 (1943).

10. Salvail v. Nashua Board of Education, 469 F. Supp. 1269 (D.N.H. 1979).

11. Right to Read Defense Committee v. School Committee of the City of Chelsea, 454 F. Supp. 703 (D. Mass. 1978).

12. Miami Herald v. Tornillo, 418 U.S. 241 (1974).

13. Cary v. Board of Education, 427 F. Supp. 945 (D. Colo. 1978), aff'd on other grounds, 598 F.2d 535 (10th Cir. 1979).

14. New York Times Co. v. United States, 403 U.S. 713 (1971).

15. 357 U.S. 116 (1958).

16. Virginia State Board of Pharmacy v. Virginia Consumer Council, 425 U.S. 748 (1976).

17. Presidents Council, District 25 v. Community School Board No. 25, 457 F.2d 289 (2d Cir. 1972).

18. Minarcini v. Strongsville City School District, 541 F.2d 577 (6th Cir. 1976).

19. 563 F.2d 512 (2d Cir. 1977), cert denied, 435 U.S. 925 (1978).

20. Tinker v. Des Moines Independent Community School District, 393 U.S. 503 (1969).

21. FCC v. Pacifica, 438 U.S. 726 (1978).

22. 372 U.S. 58 (1963).

23. Writers Guild of America West, Inc. v. FCC, 423 F. Supp. 1064 (C.D. Cal. 1976), vacated and remanded sub nom. Writers Guild of America v. American Broadcasting Co., 609 F.2d 355 (9th Cir. 1979), cert denied, 101 S. Ct. 85 (1980).

24. Wexner v. Anderson Union High School District Board of Trustees, Superior Court Case no. 61542. Appeal pending, Third Appellate District Case no. 20681.

SCHOOLBOOK CENSORSHIP LITIGATION

1. The only exception was the preparation of a brief, *amicus curiae* in the *Pico* case, on behalf of a number of academic organizations.

2. See Cary v. Board of Education, 598 F.2d 535, 539-43 (10th Cir. 1979); Loewen v. Turnipseed, 488 F. Supp. 1138, 1151 (N.D. Miss. 1980).

3. In Right to Read Defense Committee of Chelsea v. School Committee, 454 F. Supp. 703 (D. Mass. 1978), e.g., Judge Tauro held parents did not have standing to object to the removal of books from a high school library. I think he was right.

4. Pico v. Board of Education, Island Trees Union Free School District, 638 F.2d 404 (2d Cir. Oct. 2, 1980).

5. Bicknell v. Vergennes Union High School Board of Directors, 638 F.2d 438 (2d Cir. Oct. 2, 1980).

6. Right to Read Defense Committee of Chelsea v. School Committee, 454 F. Supp. 703 (D. Mass. 1978).

7. Loewen v. Turnipseed, 488 F. Supp. 1138 (N.D. Miss. 1980).

8. 469 F. Supp. 1269 (D.N.H. 1979).

9. Presidents Council, District No. 25 v. Community School Board No. 25, 457 F. 2d 289 (2d Cir.), cert denied, 409 U.S. 998 (1972).

10. 425 U.S. 748, 756. See also Procunier v. Martinez, 416 U.S. 396 (1974); Kleindienst v. Mandell, 408 U.S. 753 (1972); Red Lion Broadcasting v. FCC, 395 U.S. 367 (1969).

11. 393 U.S. 503, 509 (1969).

12. 541 F.2d 577, 582 (6th Cir. 1976).

13. Cary v. Board of Education, 598 F.2d 535 (10th Cir. 1979).

14. If one is making this argument, a claim under 42 U.S.C. 1981 might well be added, as it was in that case, providing a cause of action for racial discrimination.

15. FCC v. Pacifica Foundation, 438 U.S. 726 (1978).

A FIRST AMENDMENT PERSPECTIVE

1. Minarcini v. Strongsville City School District, 541 F.2d 577 (6th Cir. 1976).

2. Right to Read Defense Committee v. School Committee of the City of Chelsea, 454 F. Supp. 703 (D. Mass. 1978).

3. Minarcini v. Strongsville City School District, note 1 *supra*.

CURRENT AND FUTURE LITIGATION

1. Indianapolis School Commissioners v. Jacobs, 420 U.S. 128 (1975).

2. 402 F. Supp. 1039 (E.D. pa. 1975), vacated and remanded *sub nom.* Kremens v. Bartley, 431 U.S. 119 (1977).

3. Right to Read Defense Committee v. School Committee of Chelsea, 454 F. Supp. 703 (D. Mass. 1978).

4. Presidents Council, District 25 v. Community School Board No. 25, 457 F.2d 289 (2d Cir. 1972).

5. Miami Herald v. Tornillo, 418 U.S. 241 (1974).

6. PruneYard Shopping Center v. Robins, 447 U.S. 74 (1980).

7. Salvail v. Nashua Board of Education, 469 F. Supp. 1269 (D.N.H. 1979).

8. 524 F.2d 862 (3d Cir. 1975), on remand, 469 F. Supp. 773 (D.N.J. 1978) and 471 F. Supp. 166 (D.N.J. 1979).